NLP
Made Easy

❖ Also in the Made Easy series ❖

The Akashic Records

Animal Communication

Astrology

Chakras

Connecting with the Angels

Connecting with the Fairies

Crystals

Discovering Your Past Lives

Energy Healing

Feng Shui

Goddess Wisdom

Lucid Dreaming

Meditation

Mediumship

Mindfulness

Numerology

Qabalah

Reiki

Self-Hypnosis

Shamanism

Tantra

Tarot

NLP

Made Easy

How to Use Neuro-Linguistic
Programming to Change Your Life

ALI CAMPBELL

HAY HOUSE

Carlsbad, California • New York City
London • Sydney • New Delhi

Published in the United Kingdom by:
Hay House UK Ltd, The Sixth Floor, Watson House,
54 Baker Street, London W1U 7BU
Phone: +44 (0)20 3927 7290 • Fax: +44 (0)20 3927 7291
www.hayhouse.co.uk

Published in the United States of America by:
Hay House Inc., PO Box 5100, Carlsbad, CA 92018-5100
Tel: (1) 760 431 7695 or (800) 654 5126
Fax: (1) 760 431 6948 or (800) 650 5115
www.hayhouse.com

Published in Australia by:
Hay House Australia Ltd, 18/36 Ralph St, Alexandria NSW 2015
Tel: (61) 2 9669 4299; Fax: (61) 2 9669 4144
www.hayhouse.com.au

Published in India by:
Hay House Publishers India, Muskaan Complex, Plot No.3, B-2,
Vasant Kunj, New Delhi 110 070
Tel: (91) 11 4176 1620; Fax: (91) 11 4176 1630
www.hayhouse.co.in

This book was previously published as *NLP* (*Hay House Basics* series).
ISBN: 978-1-78180-353-0

A catalogue record for this book is available from the British Library.

ISBN: 978-1-4019-6663-8

Interior illustrations: 16, 21, 22, 95, 121, 134 © Ali Campbell;
all other illustrations © istockphoto.com

Printed in the United States of America

Dedicated to everyone who has sought and hoped for change in themselves and others. Everything comes from nothing more than the thought of what might be possible. It's a simple spark of magic that starts from within, but it can change the world.

Contents

List of Exercises

Acknowledgements

There are a great many people who make a book possible. Some you'd expect and many more, too many to name, who in their own way add a word, an idea, spark a thought or lend a hand. Thank you to all my students and clients over the years who have taught me as much as I have taught them, and to all who have touched my life in a positive way over the course of this project. But there are very special thanks due to a few, without whom this book wouldn't have been possible.

Dr Richard Bandler for his life's work that is NLP and for making fast, effective change accessible to all.

John Grinder also for his part in the creation of a field that has changed my own life and the lives of thousands.

Paul McKenna for all my early learnings and for igniting the spark in me all those years ago in London.

Michael Neill who really helped me to 'get it' and to try again if I didn't. 'I don't know... let's find out' is what I've spent ten years doing to great effect.

A great big heartfelt thank you to everyone at Hay House but particularly Michelle Pilley, Jo Burgess, Julie Oughton, Carolyn Thorne and Amy Kiberd for all your love and support of me personally and for all the work you do shining light in our world.

Thank you also to my amazing editor Sandy Draper for making sense of it all, again!

And finally thank you to my wife Claire for all your love and support, not to mention all the cups of tea and cuddles. Love you with all my heart, forever and for keeps.

Introduction

A Catalyst for Change

So what is NLP and why should you take the time to read the whole of this book and allow it to change the way you experience yourself and the world around you?

Let me be very upfront and say that I am not one of those 'this book will change your life; you've been doing it all wrong' guys. I'm sure, just like me, you have been doing your best too. Different circumstances and different choices for sure, but when it comes down to it, we've been doing our best given our circumstances, experiences and the available choices we perceived at the time. We look at the world around us and pick the best path we can imagine to get through it and, at the same time, try to collect some of what we want along the way, right?

I certainly did. Long before I had ever heard of NLP – like most people, I suspect – I viewed the world as being a more or less static place where things were as they were and change... well, that was hard and definitely happened only on the outside, out there in the physical world, and usually for other people, not people like me.

Now think about it. It is really quite difficult to change the world around us, isn't it? In the world of form and physics, change can be very hard indeed and takes a great deal of effort, but that, in itself, is not really the problem. The problem is rarely actually found in the physical world but rather in our subjective experience of it. As super coach Michael Neill describes it, 'We're not scared of what we think we're afraid of, we're afraid of what we think.'

Really, think about it for a second... Some people are scared of spiders and some people are not, while others are scared of dogs and cats or flying or even baked beans and ketchup... But most of us are not, so those things simply cannot, in and of themselves, be inherently scary. It MUST be our thoughts *about* those things that create those feelings of anxiety and sometimes even blind panic.

It's as simple as that. We don't need to change the world when we can effortlessly change the way we *perceive* the world out there, and in doing so change 'our' world instantly. Whilst change in the world of form and physics takes time and effort, in the world of thought and mind we are only ever one different thought away from being OK.

All human behaviour is a product of the state of mind we are in at the time. The difference between being in 'a right state' and 'the right state' is right there between your ears right now. Over the course of this book, I am going to show you how to make the small changes on the inside that will make huge differences on the outside, because when you change your mind you change your life.

Imagine tomorrow, not feeling afraid, not blocked by irrational fears from doing the things you want, not craving foods that don't serve you but only feed an emotional hunger, not feeling stuck or frustrated and instead just feeling free to be you, the authentic you, and free not just being you but free *by* just being you. Imagine as you read this book just how much your life can change when you get out of your own way and start to live up to your fullest potential.

That's really what NLP is all about; you, and how you run your own mind and put a twinkle in your eye as you do it.

Ahead for change

At school we are taught *what* to think, but we are never taught *how* to think, until now, that is. The world where we live is changing so fast that, while in the past IQ and knowledge were where all the power sat, now we are never more than a few simple clicks away from the factual answer. That being the case, how we use our brains must change too. No longer do you have to use your brain as a hard drive; now, it is how you use your brain, not what you store in it, that really matters.

Think of your mind more as a browser than a hard drive. So many more variables and so many more wonderful ways to use it, it's time to put you in control, again. You are never more than a few seconds away from any factual answer – no one is – so your advantage in life is not going to be found there. How you use your brain is what matters today and tomorrow and for the rest of your life.

That's what I am going to show you: how to use your brain effectively for the change and life you want and to do that with the same 'twinkle in the eye' way that for me epitomizes NLP, its ethos and methodology. If you try something and it doesn't work, try something else; simple. There is no such thing as failure here. If I want to get a client into a good state so I can help them to change then I'll make them laugh for real and anchor that real emotion, not get them to recall some dim and distant memory in such a clinical, dull way as to render it meaningless.

Sure there is a lot about NLP that cannot be 'proven' or measured in double-blind clinical trials, but stand-up comedy doesn't work under laboratory conditions either, yet we all enjoy a good laugh. No matter what the men in white coats might say, this stuff works in the real world. So open your mind and it will be my pleasure to be your guide as I hand you the instruction manual to your own mind before taking you through it: to make you not just smarter, but also different; your experience of life richer with more distinctions and in higher definition; and the journey here not just a fun learning one, but one by which you change from the inside out with NLP.

Plain and simple, these techniques and truths will change your life so, if you're ready, let's get started and see where heading towards your full potential now takes you.

I don't make any claim that the principles and techniques you will learn here are mine; they are the collective works of a great many experts and visionaries over the years. Nor is this a definitive work as, in truth, I only have the scope here to scratch the surface. This book could be many times thicker and more involved, but I hope it will whet your interest and ignite your curiosity to then go on and explore the Resources section at the end of the book.

Like any body of work, NLP has also evolved over time, but here's my version of some great old songs, which – while they stay true to the original – are original enough in themselves and with a new inside-out perspective to add some extra value to the piece. Or so I hope... as you join me on a plain and simple tour of what I think are some of the most important and potent patterns and principles in Neuro-Linguistic Programming and beyond.

Part I

THE FOUNDATIONS OF NLP

'Finding the difference that makes the difference.'
RICHARD BANDLER

Chapter 1

NLP at a Glance

How long does it take you to change your mind about something? A day? A week? A month? Longer? No, not at all, we can actually change our minds very quickly indeed. Sure, we might procrastinate and put it off for a while. We might think about it a lot, even tell ourselves stories about it, and find evidence for us being right. We might endlessly chat it over with friends and on and on and on, but when it actually comes down to it, we change our minds quickly – in a heartbeat – and so, in exactly the same way, natural, permanent and effective change only ever happens fast, just like that.

How does NLP work?

Neuro-Linguistic Programming (NLP) is a method of influencing our brain's behaviour (the 'neuro' part of Neuro-Linguistic Programming) through the use of language (the 'linguistic' part) and other types of communication to enable us to 'recode' the way our brain responds to stimuli (that's the 'programming') and enjoy new and better, more appropriate behaviours.

NLP could best be described as a hybrid of techniques – a collection of the best bits, or an ensemble, of what works best from many other therapeutic disciplines – underpinned by some core principles, such as that change happens fast and we are separate from our behaviours. In the same way that two computers can run two different programs – and in effect be two different products – while at their core only the hardware (our head) is fixed; the programming (our behaviours) is completely interchangeable. NLP often incorporates both hypnosis and self-hypnosis too, to help achieve the desired change (or 'programming').

NLP Know-how

Dr Richard Bandler invented the term 'Neuro-Linguistic Programming' in the 1970s, and was recently asked to write the definition of NLP for the *Oxford English Dictionary*, which reads: 'A model of interpersonal communication chiefly concerned with the relationship between successful patterns of behaviour and the subjective experiences (*esp.* patterns of thought) underlying them'; and 'A system of alternative therapy based on this which seeks to educate people in self-awareness and effective communication, and to change their patterns of mental and emotional behaviour.'

So NLP is fundamentally two things:

1. A way of modelling successful patterns of behaviour so that they can be replicated.

2. A form of therapy rooted in the subject's self-awareness and thought processes.

Or, in plain English, NLP is the art and science of excellence, derived from studying how top people in different fields obtain their outstanding results; and also a therapy based on shining a light of awareness on the internal processes and programs so that we can change. The good news is that anyone can learn these communication skills and improve their effectiveness, both personally and professionally.

The beginnings of NLP

NLP began in the early 1970s as a simple university thesis project in Santa Cruz, California. Then student, Richard Bandler, and his professor, John Grinder, wanted to develop models of human behaviour to understand why certain people seemed to be excellent at what they did, while others found the same tasks very challenging or nearly impossible to accomplish – all other things being equal, of course.

Inspired by pioneers in different fields of therapy and personal growth and development, Bandler and Grinder began to develop systematic procedures and theories that formed the foundations of what we know today as NLP.

The early focus of NLP was on modelling. In other words, if you do something really well and I do exactly the same as you, then we will both get the same result. Logically it makes sense, but how? Clearly, it is our mind that drives our body so what do we need to do differently in our mind to get a different result from our body?

Fascinated by the world of therapy, Bandler and Grinder began by studying three top therapists: Virginia Satir, a family therapist, who was able to get extraordinary results and consistently resolve difficult family relationships, which many other therapists found impossible; innovative psychotherapist Fritz Perls, who founded the school of therapy known as Gestalt therapy; and then, famously, the great Milton Erickson, the world's leading hypnotherapist.

Their goal was to develop models of how these three therapists got results so fast. The concept of modelling is a very simple principle and so they focused on the *how* by identifying and modelling the patterns or techniques that consistently produced these outstanding results. The acid test of this modelling being that they would then be able to teach these models to others and get the same results – even without any of the original therapists' background skill, experience or knowledge.

These three very gifted therapists were also very different personalities and ascribed to very different modalities of change, yet Grinder and Bandler discovered some powerful underlying patterns in their work that were very similar. It was these key patterns or techniques that became the foundation structure of NLP as we know it today, and many of the well-known NLP phrases – e.g. meta model, submodalities, reframing, language patterns, well-formed outcomes, conditions and eye-accessing cues – all come from this very early formulation period.

It's not known, or perhaps just not remembered, when the phrase 'Neuro-Linguistic Programming' was first used to describe the process of how personality creates and expresses itself. But when Bandler and Grinder started teaching NLP it's reported that the first class of students quickly nicknamed it 'Mindf**k 101'. Fortunately, the nickname didn't stick or the world of therapy could be a very different place.

NLP: the fundamental principles

NLP works on the principle that humans are made up of a neurology that conveys information about our environment to the central nervous system and brain. Since we are also meaning-creating creatures, we have to *make sense* of things in order to know what to do with them, so we translate these perceptions into meanings, beliefs and then expectations.

As we grow from a baby into a more complex adult human, we tend to filter, distort and magnify the input we get from our environment so that it matches the elaborate program we've evolved to explain our life experiences to ourselves.

As infants, we pass through the 'magical thinking' phase, and various other stages of development, on our journey to adulthood. Magical thinking is most dominantly present in children aged between two and seven years. During this time, children strongly believe that their personal thoughts have a direct effect on the rest of the world. Therefore if they experience something tragic they don't understand, for example a death, their mind creates a reason to feel responsible. Jean Piaget, a developmental psychologist, came up with the theory of four developmental stages, and children aged between two and seven years are classified under his 'Preoperational Stage' of development. During this stage children are perceived not to be able to use logical thinking. Their young minds don't understand the finality of an event like death, and so magical thinking bridges the gap.

The study of how we do all this at all ages, the kinds of meanings we make up from our perceptions and the internal programming and external behaviours we set up to explain, predict and make sense of it all – this is what the core of NLP is all about.

NLP Know-how

In NLP, we are not so much interested in *why* we do what we do, but *how*. The *why* part relates to history and the meaning we give it, but we can't change history. It also relates to people trying to do the best they could at the time and subsequently, given their frame of reference, the experience filters that they are passing the information through and also the best options they 'think' they have in the moment. For the most part, people are generally trying to do their best. Very few deliberately set out to be assholes (although many achieve it), but most people are simply doing the best they can, given all those factors. For that reason, *how* someone constructs their subjective experience is far more useful than *why* they do so, not to mention far easier to change – and with far more variables, and therefore options, for different outcomes than anything else we have to work with.

NLP in other therapies

Today, NLP has grown in a myriad different directions, including hypnosis and behavioural, personal change work and structures of beliefs, as well as modelling personal success, systems of excellence, expertise in business coaching and sales training. It has been 'popularized' by the remarkable works of luminaries such as Paul McKenna, John La Valle, Robert Dilts, Tad James, Tony Robbins,

Michael Neill, Eric Robbie, Phil Parker and, of course, Dr Richard Bandler himself. Richard, to be absolutely correct, is credited as the co-creator of NLP. His then professor, John Grinder, has also developed their creation further as Richard still does, but it's the Bandler school of thought that has really shaped NLP as most people know it.

In my own work as a therapist and life coach, NLP is just what I do. As a result, my understanding has deepened as to the nature of our subjective experience. I'd like to think that some of what you're learning here is akin to being given the TV remote to your brain: you can make the horror movie less scary and, in fact, even change the channel to something that makes you feel good. But it *is* worth mentioning that what you see, think and believe in your head is just a movie and when you stop engaging with it – stop believing it and acting as though it were true – you automatically go back to your default setting (which is happy) anyway.

There really is nothing you need to do to *make* yourself happy. Happiness is just what happens when you do less on the inside, not more. Just as the nature of water is clear, you don't need to do anything to make it clearer, or keep it clean, it is just clear. If, for any reason, it's not, then the best way to return it to clarity is not finding a new way to shake it or stir it up, but to leave it alone. And that is exactly the same with you. You have an innate clarity, an innate wellbeing and an innate knowing. Sure, sometimes your thoughts get in the way, and you will find some great techniques in the following chapters to help you when they do, but they work in the same way that a dressing on a cut provides a clean environment for it to heal. In other words, it is not the dressing that *does* the healing, it is you; the dressing simply helps you to heal and returns you to your natural setting of wellness.

I am delighted and grateful to Dr Bandler for the impact that NLP has had on my life and the lives of the countless people I have been able to help. Giving someone the control they are looking for is a priceless gift, just as being able to adjust the movie and live a different life is a special thing. However, realizing that you are already OK and knowing when you stay out of your own way for long enough you tend to do just great, is a profound and life-changing insight for most people – perhaps now for you too.

Applications of NLP

As I alluded to earlier, aspects of NLP have also been incorporated into other therapies too, such as EMDR (eye movement desensitization and reprocessing). NLP has also been taken in a more spiritual direction and used to assist in the alignment of personal behaviours and beliefs with a higher purpose and connection to the Divine and spirit. Some have even developed processes to speed healing in hospital settings and to lessen the need for anaesthesia during medical procedures. NLP techniques have also been applied to influencing sales and negotiations, and even how to pick up women. You name it, there's probably an NLP-related application for it and a book about it too, but here we'll be focusing on its therapeutic applications, where it's proved so successful.

Take phobias, for example, an easy and illustrative choice. A phobia could be defined as 'an irrational fear' and so if it is 'irrational' then it has to be a product of our subjective experience because there is no rational basis for it, but we *think* there is... So, for instance, public speaking is listed as the second biggest fear after death, which means that almost as many people would be as scared of giving the eulogy at a funeral as they would be of being in the casket itself.

NLP has proved incredibly successful in treating irrational fears, as well as issues such as stage fright, parenting, allergies and trauma. In fact the list of areas where training in NLP and individual therapeutic work with NLP practitioners is valuable is endless – and that is simply because NLP is not about any of these specific things but about people. The hardware is more or less the same in each of us, it's the software that is variable and this can be reprogrammed quickly and easily with NLP, often just by pressing the 'restore factory settings' option and allowing us to be OK.

Eye-accessing cues

So, if you'll pardon the pun, let's start by looking at one of most well-known, if controversial, discoveries in NLP, but also potentially one of the most valuable to the novice NLPer: the observation of eye movements as indicators of specific cognitive processes.

Learning to read 'eye-accessing cues', as they are called, is a fairly simple skill and you'll probably already know that when speaking to someone their eyes tend to move all over the place. Whilst it is socially acceptable, and even expected, to look the other person in the eye, we just can't seem to do that *and* think at the same time. It's almost as if we have to look away in order to be able to access our thoughts. I distinctly remember at school (and I wasn't at all good at school stuff) being asked a question, quickly followed by the teacher barking at me that the answers weren't on the ceiling. For some reason, my eyes had drifted up whilst I was genuinely trying to think – well, before I was interrupted, that is – and when I had to look at her, I just couldn't think at all. My mind went blank, even though I knew that I knew the answer; it was on the tip of my tongue, if only I could get to it.

I'm sure you've had a similar experience, or will have certainly noticed people's eyes moving around when you've had a conversation. But have you ever noticed *how* they move?

Imagine in your mind's eye that you have a screen much like that on your computer. You know that you need to move the little cursor around to access different files on your computer. Well, it's exactly the same in your mind, only your eyes are like the cursor and the files are all arranged nice and neatly so you don't need to search around too much. The reason that my eyes naturally drifted upwards to find the answer to the question is that I am predominantly visual and had stored the answer – or at least the image to access the answer – not on the ceiling (that would be cheating), but in the folder of images that we all access by looking up. You'll have seen people do that and then perhaps say 'let me see', as they 'look' for the answer.

For a right-handed person, images that are memories tend to be up and to the left. Without looking, quickly, which side is the handle on your front door? Notice where your eyes go to access the information. Images from which we must construct the answer tend to be up and to the right. So, just imagine an elephant crossed with a rhino... where did you look? Up and right?

(But what do you call an elephant crossed with a rhino? 'Eleph – I – no'? Sorry, couldn't resist!)

Play with visual cues

Ask yourself the following, and just notice where your eyes go, then get some of your friends to do the same:

❖ Think of the colour of your car... what does the badge look like?

❖ What pattern is on your bedspread?

❖ Think of the last time you saw someone running, what did they look like?

❖ Who were the first five people you saw this morning?

All these questions are designed to make you access your visual memory, which means, for right-handed people, the eyes should go up and left.

Like most things, eye-accessing cues are not new, but rather brought together from somewhere else to give a 'best of breed' solution. The notion that eye movements might be related to internal representations was first suggested way back by American psychologist William James in his book *Principles of Psychology*. Observing that some forms of micro movement always accompany thought, James wrote:

> 'In attending to either an idea or a sensation belonging to
> a particular sense-sphere, the movement is the adjustment
> of the sense-organ, felt as it occurs. I cannot think in
> visual terms, for example, without feeling a fluctuating
> play of pressures, convergences, divergences, and
> accommodations in my eyeballs... When I try to remember
> or reflect, the movements in question... feel like a sort of
> withdrawal from the outer world. As far as I can detect,
> these feelings are due to an actual rolling outwards and
> upwards of the eyeballs.[1]

What James is describing is well known in NLP as visual eye-accessing cues, but his observation lay dormant until the early 1970s when psychologists[2-4] first began to equate lateral eye movements with processes related to the different hemispheres of the brain. They observed that right-handed people tended to shift their heads and eyes to the right during 'left hemisphere' (logical and verbally oriented) tasks, and move their heads and eyes to the left during 'right hemisphere' (artistic and spatially oriented) tasks. That is, people tended to look in the opposite direction of the part of the brain they were using to complete a cognitive task.

Then, in early 1976, Richard Bandler, John Grinder and their students began to explore the relationship between eye movements and the different senses, as well as the different cognitive processes associated with the brain hemispheres.[5]

But in 1977, Robert Dilts at the Langley Porter Neuropsychiatric Institute in San Francisco took it all a step further, when he attempted to correlate eye movements to particular cognitive and neurophysiological processes. Dilts used electrodes to track both the eye movements and brainwave characteristics of subjects who were asked questions related to using the various senses of sight, hearing and feeling for tasks involving both memory (right-brain processing) and mental construction (left-brain processing).

Subjects were asked a series of questions in eight groupings. Each grouping of questions appealed to a particular type of cognitive processing; what we know as visual, auditory and kinaesthetic (feelings). Each was also geared to either memory (non-dominant hemisphere processing) or construction (dominant hemisphere processing). Dilts' recordings tended to confirm other tests that showed that eye movements accompanied brain activity during different cognitive tasks. This pattern also seemed to hold for tasks requiring different senses.[6-7]

As a result of these and other studies[8-9] – and many hours of observations of people from different cultures and racial backgrounds from all over the world – the following eye-movement patterns were identified.

From the person's perspective

❖ **Eyes up and left:** Non-dominant hemisphere visualization – visual recall or remembered (Vr)

❖ **Eyes up and right:** Dominant hemisphere visualization – visual constructed (Vc)

❖ **Eyes lateral left:** Non-dominant hemisphere auditory processing – auditory recall or remembered (Ar); and also tonal discrimination

- ❖ **Eyes lateral right:** Dominant hemisphere auditory processing – auditory constructed (Ac)

- ❖ **Eyes down and left:** Internal dialogue, or inner self-talk, sometimes referred to as auditory digital (Ad)

- ❖ **Eyes down and right:** Feelings, both tactile and visceral – kinaesthetic (K)

- ❖ **Eyes straight ahead, but defocused or dilated:** For quick access to almost any sensory information, but usually visual

The diagram below illustrates the basic NLP eye-accessing cues.

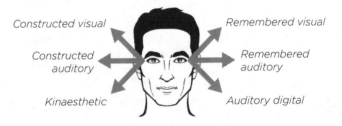

Constructed visual   Remembered visual

Constructed auditory   Remembered auditory

Kinaesthetic   Auditory digital

This pattern appears to be constant for right-handed people throughout the human race, with the possible exception of inhabitants of the Basque region who, interestingly but completely inexplicably, appear to offer a fair number of exceptions to the rule – definitely one for an NLP pop quiz.

Many left-handed people, however, tend to be reversed from left to right. That is, their eye-accessing cues are the mirror image of those of the average right-handed person. They look down and left for feelings, instead of down and right. Similarly, they look up and to the right to remember visual imagery, instead of up and to the left, and so on.

A small number of people (including ambidextrous and a few right-handed people) will be reversed in some of their eye-accessing cues (their visual eye movements, for example), but not the others.

Further exploring visual cues

To explore the relationship between eye movements and thinking, have a play with these eye-accessing cues. It's definitely easier if you find a partner; just ask the following questions and observe their eyes.

We've practised the first visual cues (see page 13) already, but for completeness, they are included in this exercise as well.

Visual recall

❖ Think of the colour of your car.

❖ What pattern is on your bedspread?

❖ Think of the last time you saw someone laughing.

❖ Who was the first man you saw this morning?

❖ Who was the first woman you saw this morning?

Visual constructed

❖ Imagine your house, but with pink and blue spots on the roof.

❖ Can you imagine the top half of a teddy bear on the bottom half of a mermaid?

Auditory recall

❖ Can you think of one of your favourite songs?

❖ Think of the sound of people clapping and cheering.

❖ How does your car's engine sound?

Auditory constructed

❖ Imagine the sound of children playing changing into the sound of your mother's voice.

❖ Imagine the national anthem played on a tambourine.

❖ Imagine what the silence of being deep in outer space would sound like.

Auditory digital (internal self-talk)

❖ Just take a moment and listen to the sound of your own inner voice. How do you know that it's your voice?

❖ In what types of situations do you talk to yourself the most?

❖ Think of the kinds of things that you say to yourself most often.

❖ Do you refer to yourself as 'you' or me' when you do?

Kinaesthetic recall (feelings remembered)

❖ When was the last time you felt really wet? Were you cold or warm?

❖ Imagine the feeling of snow in your hands.

❖ What does a wet dog feel like?

❖ When was the last time you touched something hot?

❖ Can you think of a time you felt satisfied about something you completed?

❖ Think of what it feels like to be exhausted.

❖ When was the last time you felt really curious?

Kinaesthetic construction (feelings constructed)

❖ Imagine the feeling of stickiness turning into the feelings of sand shifting between your fingers and then to ice.

❖ Imagine the feelings of frustration turning into the feeling of being really motivated to do something and then imagine the feeling of being bored turning into feeling silly about your feeling bored and then turning into curiosity again.

Creatures of habit

We all have far more scope for expression than most of us ever use, and also far more versatility and ability to change how we feel in any given moment. The problem is that we have it lined up in the wrong way a lot of the time, and so we generally just don't appreciate how many *shades* there are or how many *distinctions* we are able to make whenever we want. We humans are creatures of habit and we tend to redo things the way we have always done them... why?

Well, for the same reason that, even though all that information has been there all along, you just didn't know any better. But as soon as you notice for the first time what's there, then you can't *un-notice* it and it will always be there for you to use. The world and the people in it have always been like that; you've just never noticed before.

However, there are two small yet vital points of caution:

1. I have often heard it said when talking about eye-accessing cues that it's a good way to know when someone is lying. It *can* be, but you certainly need to consider a lot of other factors before jumping to that conclusion.

2. While the pattern described on pages 15–16 works most of the time for most right-handed people and swaps over for left-handed people, the key is in the word

'most'. Most of the time this is true, but some of the time it is not. You need to pay attention to other factors so that you get it right all of the time.

Calibration

If I am working in almost any capacity with someone, I almost always begin by making chitchat about what they did at the weekend and what they'll be doing later – nothing major, just day-to-day small talk. It seems very normal and natural, and people certainly don't think anything of it. BUT this is actually when I am paying the most attention because, in actual fact, I'm calibrating to them. What they got up to last weekend, the way they describe it and where their eyes go gives me a very good calibration reference point for how they recall information.

We have to assume that they are telling the truth, of course, but we'll take that as a given because they certainly have no reason to lie to me. Then what they are doing for the rest of the day tells me how they 'construct' information, as they have to do so in order to be able to make sense of what's coming next. Be a little careful because if that's somewhere they go or have been to before, they might have to access a memory in order to create the frame into which they can then place the scene.

However, you'll notice that I have asked 'what' they are doing later, not where they will be going, so usually, after a brief foray into the past to get the scene set, they will be over on the right side constructing and giving me another really useful calibration reference point. You might also like to notice on which wrist they wear their watch (although this is increasingly less reliable) or which hand they write with to know which is their dominant hand. The second point is that even once you're sure of how they are 'wired up', be careful before jumping to the conclusion that someone might be lying. We need to be very careful and clean with the questions that we ask.

Case study

I was once sitting in, assisting on an interview panel to select some very senior managers for an organization, and when one candidate left the room, the HR person turned to me and said, 'I think he was the best so far; it's a real pity he was lying.' There then ensued a very long conversation about how they knew that from the person's eye-accessing cues. (She had been on a one-day NLP course and thought she had it sussed.) Here's the question she asked and here's how his eyes moved... Can you spot where she went wrong?

'In your previous role with XYZ Corporation, what was a key skill that you developed, the one that gave the biggest results, and how would you be able to utilize that experience here?'

His eyes did this... for a split second.

Remembered visual

Then this as he answered.

Constructed visual

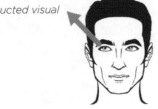

When challenged, the HR person said that she knew for certain that he was lying because he looked up and right the entire time when answering, only occasionally looking at her and then 'furtively' (as she put it) looking away and up and right, which showed he was lying.

What she hadn't factored in, however, was that while in her head, her line of questioning was rooted in what the candidate would bring to her company based on his last job (and he did access up and left to find that memory, but only for a split second), the majority of the thinking required to answer the question accurately actually required him to construct an answer placed in the future. Given that he had never worked for that company and had therefore never used any of his skills there, never mind that one, the only possible way to form an answer was to project what he did know into that situation and to keep doing so until he felt he had given as complete an account as his imagination would allow him to construct. Which is exactly what he did.

What the interviewer mistook for looking 'furtively' away from her eye contact was actually the candidate quickly getting back to his picture under interview pressure to continue with his answer before he lost his train of thought. She completely missed the 'up and left' visual-recall accessing cue. After clearing that up, the guy got the job! Of course, what would have helped would have been if our candidate had been able to build better rapport in the first place. Although I'm sure it wouldn't have prevented the HR person from getting it wrong, she would have been much more likely to give him the benefit of the doubt.

This chapter has been all about noticing what's always been there, but that you've just never noticed before. I wonder where else that might be true in your life? Yes, take away what you have learned about eye movements and accessing cues from here, but there's a much bigger 'take away' too. The more you turn up your own sensory acuity, and the more you pay attention to the world and those around you, the more options you have, both in what to do and how to be next.

Chapter 2

The Mind: A Browser, Not a Hard Drive

When most of us think about our mind, we tend to think of it in the way that we are conditioned to use it through education: as a place where we store information. The smarter ones amongst us are the ones who can recall that information in, more or less, the same form as it went in and so we are able to pass exams that are set predominantly as a test of memory and the application of that memory.

Perhaps, as I mentioned in the previous chapter, it's because when I was growing up, I wasn't very good at that, but to me it just never seemed like a particularly good way to measure smartness. I knew many people who were straight-A students but couldn't wire a plug or solve a basic life problem, or who, despite having a brain the size of a planet, just couldn't get along with people or apply that knowledge in the real world in a way that helped them navigate their own course any better or with fewer mistakes than anyone else.

Even growing up, the problem seemed really obvious to me: education is about fixed, solid facts for the most part whereas life is about thoughts, emotions and people. But thoughts and emotions are not fixed and so nor are the answers. IQ is what gets you through school, but EQ (emotional intelligence) is what gets you through life.

Upgrading your search

This is a book to help you not just get through your life, but thrive! And so we need to think about the mind very differently. Your mind is much more like an Internet browser than a hard drive. Sure, we can cache information for easy access, but just like your browser, if you don't open it for a while, you lose it. Yes, we all have a history but it can be cleared, and we are all able to search and find the information we need. It's *how* we do that which really matters and makes the difference – how we search for and find what we are looking for.

Let's take this analogy just a little further. Back in the dark ages, when the Internet was but a child, when we didn't find what we were looking for on the first page of Google, Yahoo, Excite, MSN, AOL or whichever of the many different browsers our dial-up modem (very slowly) took us to – with the horrible electronic noise as the soundtrack for our journey into cyber space – we would click on the second, third, fourth, fifth page trying to find what we were looking for.

Now, think about the way the Internet has evolved. It's always on, always available, the answer is right there in your pocket and when you search, if you don't find what you are looking for, you don't click down into the depths of more wrong answers trying to find the solution, you just change the search, don't you?

Now think about how you run your head; is it anything like that? Has it evolved too? No!

For the most part, we assume that what's readily at our disposal is all we've got to work with. We search based on what we have always searched for and when the same wrong answers come up, we either try them again and get the same result as before or dismiss them, knowing them to be wrong. And in doing so, we leave ourselves stuck. It's not *what* we have in our head that's the problem; it's *how* we use it.

So, let's start by changing what we are searching for. How would you like to be and what would you have in your life, even if you have no idea how to get it?

Do that right now. What is it that comes up for you? What is it that you would most like to change? Now let me pop a little caveat in right here. While we are not talking about being able to change the world around us, let me be very clear; when you make the changes in your mind, they will filter through into your environment faster than you think. That part is absolutely inevitable; it's just a given, but without starting in the right place on the inside, you will likely have just as much of a struggle as you've had until now. So let's stop that and I'll explain not only why getting the change you want is easier than you think, but also the inevitability of how it will play out for you in the real world.

It all starts with your thoughts. The problem, of course, is not that we have thoughts; the problem is that we believe them and engage with them and allow them to shape our lives. Of course, when we start on our personal development journey, we get that concept pretty quickly and, just as quickly, jump to the usual and rather inevitable conclusion that if bad thoughts equals bad things then surely the solution to feeling better is simply to think good thoughts, right? And I'll bet you've tried that already. How did that go for you?

I'm no mind-reader, but I'll bet that it went fine while you were doing it, but just like everyone (and I do mean *everyone* else), you couldn't or didn't keep it up and so went right back to where you started. Only this time with the added thought that change must be harder than you thought, harder then all those self-help gurus make it out to be. Right? Of course! Part of you wishes it was different and a big part of you wishes that *you* were different and perhaps it's that part that has caused you to keep looking till now for the solution that's right for you. Of course, you keep all this to yourself, don't you? I mean, like most people, you would very nearly die of embarrassment, if you thought the world could hear your thinking out loud.

But that's where I'm going to depress you just a little bit further: whether you like it or not, the life you are leading IS a product of your thinking.

Thought creates feelings, feelings create actions and actions create outcomes. So whether you like it or not, while the exact detail might be hidden, the world can already witness the outcome of your thinking every day, every time you leave the house or interact with someone.

Now, let me cheer you up again. The problem is not that we have thoughts; the problem is not even that they are hard to change from negative to positive and the problem is not even one that you have created. It's all just a big misunderstanding. We are taught throughout our lives that in order to make sense of things, we need to be able to explain them logically and we need to be able to apply certain laws and universal constants to them in order to be validated. The problem for those of us making changes on the inside is that we apply the wrong laws to the wrong thing.

The laws of physics don't apply in your mind

If I had a big tree root in my garden and I wanted to remove it to plant a flowerbed, I could quite reasonably expect it to be hard work. The tree is heavy, it's been there for a very long time and its roots run deeper than the foundations of my house itself. You might reasonably expect that I would need some tools and that I would need to struggle and *put my back into it* and that, if I did that consistently, I would first of all see the root start to move a little, then I might be able to use that little movement to get some leverage. From there, I might be able to break it loose from what had been keeping it stuck and then, with even more effort, I might be able to lift it out and take it away. Sounds about right, right?

Of course, this will take some time, but in our favour, we do have nature on our side. Just like going to the gym – if I kept at it and kept at it, my body, without any additional mental input from me and without my asking, would just naturally get stronger to cope with the physical strain of the load I was putting it under and help me to reach my goal. First of all, we recruit all the resources we have available in the form of additional muscle fibres and then when we need even more, those muscle fibres start to grow thicker and stronger, and that is how we build muscle.

However, when we want to make changes in our mind instead, those laws of physics and form simply do not apply and, in fact, the inverse is true. When we consistently apply an additional physical load to our body, we get stronger, but when we consistently apply an additional mental load to our mind, we get weaker. Not because it's our fault, it's just how we are made, how we are naturally wired up. The body is designed to do more on the outside and less on the inside; we just don't tend to run it like that any more... the laws of physics and form simply do not apply to the world of thoughts and mind; we just think they do, until we know better, that is.

Change doesn't have to take a long time

Think about it this way: if you have had a DVD in your collection that terrifies you every time you watch it, it doesn't matter whether you've had it for 20 years or 20 minutes, you can throw it out and be done with it just as fast.

So here's the best news: we know that it's much easier to change our mind than the world around us already. But a few weeks ago, while driving home, I was struck by yet another example of how we habitually get it all wrong when it's just as easy, in fact, even easier, to get it all sorted.

If, like me, you're a reluctant fan of all things electronic, then you will be familiar with the 'read only' message that often pops up when you try to edit a document. You have no problem accessing it; it could even be right in the forefront of your mind on your desktop, but you just can't change it; you haven't 'permission' to do so.

I had just finished fighting with one such issue and was listening to the *Richard Bacon Show* on BBC 5 Live on the radio when those same words caught my attention, 'there are no read-only files in the brain...'

I turned it up and listened carefully: 'Every time we access a memory, we change it; in all the studies, it has been found that the act of recalling a memory has the effect of distorting it in some way.' This wasn't just anyone's opinion; the voice from my dashboard was none other than that of Simon Watt, evolutionary biologist and fellow *Huffington Post* columnist. Simon knows a thing or two and, as I listened to him on the BBC that afternoon, I really got to thinking.

If every time we open a memory file we inadvertently yet automatically change it in some way, then this surely explains why, over time, with sustained attention, the problems, pain and fears we suffer do tend to get worse. It certainly explains post-traumatic stress disorder (PTSD), and even phobias and panic attacks.

Think about it; do you tend to think about your problems rather a lot? Yes, of course. But did you realize that by doing so, you are changing them and probably making them worse? I bet not...

But, if a memory changes every time we access it, then it absolutely stands to reason that we can change things for the better just as easily.

That's certainly been my experience working with literally thousands of people all over the world. Add to this the fact that our default setting is actually 'OK and happy', and it explains why I often describe my work as being like hitting 'restore factory settings', and why my clients experience change at a rate and with an ease that suggests they are not just deleting individual files, but making some profound and innate changes at a much deeper level.

All lasting change happens from the inside out and, call it what you will, it's official: 'there are no read-only files' in your mind and you can change your mind and thus change your life much faster than you think... literally!

So, knowing that and knowing that there's a large part of you that is not only just open to change but really wants it, what's stopping you? The *how to* is right here, but where do you want to start?

I would suggest, if I may, that we start where you think you will get the biggest benefit and go with that. Let's find out where the smallest of changes on the inside make the biggest difference on the outside and on the outside world.

Now I'm guessing that you picked up this book for a reason so let's start there. I don't need to know what it is (that could be tricky), but so long as *you* do, that's all that matters. You can write it down now if it helps, but if you do, make sure that you also keep it in mind as you read on. I want for this to be a meaningful conversation about you, one where you can get really clear – not on *why* you do things, I don't really care about that; after all, we can't go back and change history, can we? – but we can easily change *how* you feel about it. This is not a book about what and why; this is a book all about HOW: *how* you construct that subjective experience and *how* we can change that for you so that you automatically go back to being OK. That is your default setting, after all.

Submodalities

So *how* do you do it?

We said earlier that all human behaviour is a product of the state of mind we are in at the time, but do you know how we build those states?

Well, we build them on the inside in exactly the same way as we experience them on the outside, through our senses. We even say that we need to *make sense* of things in order to understand them. We create our internal experiences mainly in pictures, sounds and feelings. What's your favourite memory? How do you create that now? Close your eyes if it's safe to do so and notice what's there on the inside when you think about it now. It's most likely some pictures, some sounds and some feeling somewhere in your body, right? So if that is how you create that state and those 'submodalities' are the building blocks, let's go a bit further and take just a few easy examples of places we can go to change our state. In fact, let's take three of my favourites.

1. Cinema

We have all had the experience of being completely lost in a really good movie. We feel sad at the sad parts, laugh out loud at the funny parts, get ready to jump out of our skin as the tension mounts and leave with the feel-good glow of a happy ending. The pictures are big, huge, in fact, and bright and bold and obviously they are moving and sometimes, in 3D, we feel like we are right there in the action, so long as those little 3D glasses don't annoy us too much, that would distract us and ruin it. The images are so big they engulf our senses and take us to that magical state where we can suspend our disbelief and just go with it.

2. Concert

Then there's the concert hall. The mood builds as the support band works the stage. They always have a tough time because it's not their crowd, but that's not important; they are there to get the crowd ready and *'in state'* for the main event. Although, to be honest, at really big events, the main act would have to really suck from the outset not to get a good reception, because the anticipation of seeing them has been building in the audience for months, ever since they bought the album, then saw the advert for the tour and bought their tickets. All that time, the state has been building so that by the time the lead singer opens their mouth, 70,000 people are ready to burst with excitement.

The sound is big and loud and a whole team of technicians has made sure it's just right, not just so that you can hear every note perfectly; that's not what live events are really all about, but so that it *does it for you* for maximum impact on your senses. You are hearing the onslaught of audio for all it's worth, so much so that you can't hear yourself think. Have you ever heard that expression?

Well, that's because we can only process one audio track at a time. Sure we can think and have sound in the background, but we must tune in to one or the other in order to process it. Perhaps, like me, you remember sitting in the classroom thinking about what you were having for lunch or what time the pub opens when a curt, 'What was I saying?' from the teacher jolted you from your trance. Of course, you had no idea; you were listening to your voice (your thoughts), the audio channel on the inside, not the one droning on the outside about algebra or something equally dull.

So, as the concert opens and the sound booms, you can't hear yourself think for a while. But that is usually short-lived; even the very best performers in the world only have a short timeframe to impress you before your own inner critic kicks in. You may have started off in a peak state of anticipation and excitement, but if they don't deliver, then your state will quickly change as you engage more with the voice of your inner critic and less with the sound on the outside... ever had that experience? I'm sure we all have.

The legendary comedian Jerry Seinfeld reckons that even the very best have a window of about five minutes to impress or flop. Their fame and the expectations of the audience will only buy them that much time before they have to deliver the goods or they are back to square one.

3. Bed

But there is nothing quite like climbing into your own bed with crisp, freshly laundered sheets, is there? The feeling of being completely supported, of the covers gently nestling around your body as your head sinks into the pillow, and if you feel the soft warm touch of someone you love, then so much the better. Somehow, the feeling of comfort around you, beneath you and on top of you spreads right through you, enveloping you with a feeling that helps you drift all the way down into a deeply relaxing sleep. You don't have to do anything to get there; you just have to be there and the rest happens all by itself.

What does it for you?

All the senses we have on the outside are replicated on the inside. And to make sense of things, we have to *represent* them on the inside and *filter/distort* what we believe to be important about that information in order for it to fit best with our map of the world. So what is it about the cinema, a concert and snuggling up in your own bed that works so well for you?

Well, if you are predominantly visually oriented, then the cinema is really going to do it for you; the images being big and bold and bright are going to create some really powerful states in you, ones that you will be able to *re-present* for a long time to come and, when you do, they will create even more powerful states, just like thinking back to a favourite holiday or the day your children were born.

You will most likely be able to see those memories through your own eyes; you will be able to feel like you are really there and be able to mentally run the movie forward to the best bit as if you have the control of the recorded live event on the hard drive that is your mind.

If the concert does it for you then you are most probably aligned in a more auditory sense, your memories will generally feature a lot of sound and fewer pictures and if you want to change your state you'll likely listen to music or even just silence that'll make you feel good.

If the thought of snuggling up in those crisp, clean sheets does it for you then you are most likely to be more aligned around your feelings that in NLP we call 'kinaesthetic'.

While it's not accurate to group people firmly into any category, never mind whether they are 'visual', 'auditory' or 'kinaesthetic', it is true that we tend to be more dominant in one with the other two major representation systems following on behind. If you are wondering which order you work in, we'll figure that out next.

So, we have learned that all of us are dominant in one of those major internal representation systems, but there are also two more beyond the big three: taste (gustatory) and smell (olfactory), but most (unless you are a spaniel) don't navigate their way around the world using taste and smell because that would be weird! So we humans use pictures, which we will call 'visual'; we use sounds, which, of course, we call 'auditory'; and we use feelings, which in NLP, we refer to as 'kinaesthetic', to 'make sense' of the world around us and create the thoughts, feelings, emotions and choices that turn into our lives. Our lives are shaped from this very basic level of internal pictures, sounds and feelings, but there's more.

Auditory digital submodality

In addition to the three submodalities described above, there is one other factor to consider here. Not to complicate things, but 'fact-or' is in fact a really good word for it. Some people tend to be what we in NLP call 'auditory digital'. In other words, they appear to process fact but with very little in the way of accessing any other internal systems. You'll know them though; those are the people who, when you are talking to them, tend to stare straight ahead and answer in rather obvious and less subjective terms than most.

Simply put, predominantly auditory digital people deal with logic. To outline the difference between auditory and auditory digital submodalities, try out the following example and see if you can spot the difference. The first example is of an auditory digital response, whilst the second is an example of a standard auditory response.

AD: 'You have provided me with a way to proceed that makes sense to me and I would like to have more details now.'

A: 'You have told me of a way to proceed that sounds good and I would like to hear all about it.'

An auditory person may say, 'I can't hear what you are saying' or 'this doesn't sound right'. An auditory digital person may say, 'there is no logic in what you are saying' or simply, 'this does not make sense to me'.

The person who is primarily auditory digital uses words like logic, common sense, reason, system, understand, think, analyse, know, learn; and phrases like due diligence, I'll consider the idea, to sum up, to make sense of. You will notice little or no emotion in their language and very few assumptions or constructs; they are interested in the facts, just the facts. A cute trick is just to remember that something which is 'digital' is either 1 or 0, on or off. There are no shades of grey; it's either black or white.

In the next chapter, I'll explain why we are never really starting from a clean slate, but also how to change all that faster than you think. But for now think back to your favourite happy memory again and complete this framework, noticing what you notice about what's there on the inside and just as importantly what's not, the parts you have to leave blank.

Completing a submodalities checklist

VISUAL (picture)

❖ Is the picture black and white or colour?

❖ Is it near or far?

❖ Is it bright or dim?

❖ Where is it? Point to it and note its location in space.

❖ What's the size of the picture?

❖ Are you seeing it through your own eyes?

❖ Or seeing it from somewhere else?

❖ Is the picture framed or panoramic?

❖ Is it a movie or still?

❖ Is it 3D or flat?

AUDITORY (sound)

❖ Which direction is the sound coming from?

❖ Is it internal or external?

❖ Is it loud or quiet? Rate on a scale of 1–10.

❖ High or low pitch?

❖ Tonality?

❖ Quality – clear or muffled?

❖ Rhythm?

KINAESTHETIC (feeling)

❖ Location, where in your body?

❖ Size... the size of a...?

❖ Texture?

❖ Intensity?

❖ Movement, which direction?

❖ Temperature – warm or cool?

❖ Pressure and weight – heavy or light?

Now, more than ever before, 'how' you are in the world is so much more important than who you are or what you know. How you use your own mind is going to be the difference that makes all the difference. Before you start trying to use these techniques on or with anyone else, please first get to know you and how you are 'wired up', then use that new knowledge to make new choices and a new life, or at the very least, a new experience of it.

Chapter 3

Making 'Sense' of NLP

We learned in the previous chapter about our internal representation system and how different pictures, sounds and feelings affect us. But in order to assess what is important and what is not and therefore know how to *be*, we need to have some way of filtering the many thousands of pieces of information we are presented with every day. Clearly, they can't all be equally important, but what we choose to make important very much shapes our map of the world around us.

Put very simply, we take in information via those main senses – visual, auditory, kinaesthetic – and pass it through a filter of our previous personal experiences, the process of which deletes information that we perceive not to be important or relevant to us. We also distort some of it in the process and then generalize what's left in order to make it fit into one of the nice groupings we already have. We pigeonhole it, if you like, so that we know what to do with it at an internal sensory level. You may have already noticed some big differences between what you noted in the 'submodalities checklist' (*see pages 39–40*) and the reality of the event you were actually remembering, especially if you were seeing it from somewhere else, when clearly you saw it through your own eyes at the time. It also wasn't likely to be black and white or completely silent either... interesting eh? What did you notice for yourself?

Then think about it like this for a moment in a more general sense. If we're starting a conversation about cars, then, if you are visual, an image of something to do with cars probably just popped up in your mind. What was it? Because I'll bet it was very different from the image that's in my mind's eye as I write this. And it will be different in the mind's eye of every single person who ever reads this. What colour was the car? Or is the picture black and white? What make? What model? How many seats? Where is the car? How big is the picture of the car? And is it moving or still? Are you seeing it through your own eyes or from somewhere else? Is it a car you have or have had or one you'd like to own in the future? Is the picture framed or is it panoramic? Are you inside the car or outside the car? Is the picture even of a car? Or is it something to do with a car? Is it a movie called *Cars* or a movie about cars, is it motor sport or the thought of someone being knocked down by a car or of going on a journey or being stuck in traffic and being frustrated and late for work? There are all these variables and many more, but we can make them all fit rather neatly into the pigeonhole of 'cars' without even a moment's conscious thought.

The map is not the territory

In NLP, we often refer to this process with the phrase 'the map is not the territory'. It certainly *represents* the territory, but it is not the same as the real thing. Clearly, we can easily get that because, of course, a map is much smaller than the area itself; it does not have any of the features of the area but instead they are displayed using symbols, visual codes that show us what is where in relation to something else but very little of the actual detail. Even with the most accurate and detailed map, so much information is missing. Think of a map of somewhere you know really well. How accurate is it? Is each individual streetlight or paving stone marked on the map? Are you yourself on the map? No? What an oversight that is... you mean to say that all of that information has been deleted right off the map? Wow! OK, now, does the railway track go in that nice straight line and are the stations all nicely spaced at even intervals? No? So it's a distorted map then too... Well, is the local hospital at least blue and in the shape of an H? And are the roads really those colours? No? What kind of map is this? Have those things been simply generalized to make it easier for you to understand and make sense of? Exactly!

And no matter how good and detailed a map, it is always full of those deletions, distortions and generalizations... Just like the mental map of the world in your mind.

We filter out what we perceive we don't need; we distort information to make it fit and then we generalize to allow us to neatly file away that experience for storage and easy access later. But what if, instead of making the railway lines, roads and hospitals important, we chose to filter those out and focus on the trees, hills and rivers? Do you think you'd even recognize the place where you live just from those reference points on a map?

How about if you did that with a big city like London or New York? Could you navigate your way around without your usual reference points? I doubt it, but you would be in exactly the same city. Nothing at all would have changed in the real world and yet you would be completely lost without your usual reference points. Nothing has changed except what you have chosen to make important and that is exactly the same in your mind.

If you store one set of data and *re-present* it in a certain way, then you will have one experience, but as soon as you store a different set of data or hold it in a different way (about exactly the same thing), you will have a totally different experience and nothing whatsoever needs to change in the real world to make it happen. Your subjective experience can change in a heartbeat, much faster than you think, in fact. When you know how and as a good NLPer, you will have enough flexibility in your map of the world to adjust to anyone else's too... From now on, it's not anyone else's responsibility to *get you*; as NLPers, it is our responsibility to be *got*.

In Part II, you will be given all the know-how you need to make really powerful changes in your mind and therefore in your life and the lives of others too... look forward to it.

When it's not a map: Auditory dominant

But what if you are not predominantly visual? What if sounds are much more of a driver for you than pictures? Well, in that case, what I've just said would have made much less *sense* to you than to someone who is more visually oriented. Nothing wrong with that at all, it's just how you and they are wired up... If you are more auditory dominant, then it's likely the surround sound at the cinema that does it for you or the big bank of amps and speakers at the concert. You're probably the kind of person to whom the stereo in the car is just as important as the engine and you can remember a telephone conversation as though the person were speaking to you right now. You will be reading this clearly in your own voice, and in your *reading* voice at that. That is just how *you* are wired up.

Now and, just for now, read the next few lines in your really bored voice and see what effect that has on the experience of reading this book... OK, actually, that's enough of that. Now, read the next part in your most curious, fascinated kind of voice that even makes you feel like you are sitting a little further forward and really taking it all in... OK, good, and notice the difference in your state and in how much more you retain, even though, yet again, nothing has actually changed in the real world. Hear what I'm saying?

As we've said already, the vast majority of the time, the real world is not the problem; our subjective experience of it is. But we can change that so there's no problem there either; it's all good.

When it's not a map or voice: Kinaesthetic dominant

But what if pictures don't really do it for you and you struggled to see my point and, while you can read these words, you can't replay the sound of yourself reading them... but oh, how you look forward to climbing into bed tonight and all the comfortable feelings that go with it?

You are also most likely to be someone who has a lot of different textures around your home, like a leather sofa with fluffy cushions or carpet in some rooms and tiles on the floor in others and when you go shopping, you pick things up and give them a good squeeze and feel them in your hands before deciding to buy them or not. If you're that person, then you are kinaesthetically (feelings) dominant. That's absolutely fine too; there is no right and wrong here, only how you are.

We are how we are in this respect and remember that no one is 100 per cent any one representation system. We all filter the world through all our senses and representation systems, but we definitely do have an order of preference or dominance.

As you read this, you might have found that the thought of the visuals and the feelings resonated with you most. Or maybe it was the pictures and sounds that really struck a chord, or the sounds and the feelings that you were most able to get to grips with. Whatever it was, you have just learned something really important about yourself, something that we will continue to explore with the same curiosity all the way to the end of this book and beyond.

Take this quick test to see which representation system preference you have.

Defining your representation system

For this exercise, you will need a clock, a piece of paper and a pen. You'll likely already have a big clue as to how this will go from your submodalities work so far, but this will really help you define how your representation system works.

So, for the next two minutes, describe your home using only visual words. Then, for the next two minutes, use only auditory words. Then, for the next two minutes, use only kinaesthetic words and for the final two minutes use only auditory digital words.

Hint: For visual, you can describe the different colours, shapes and generally what you can see; for auditory, the different sounds and also the different thoughts you have while in your home (sounds on the inside); for kinaesthetic, different feelings or textures; and for auditory digital, you can use facts and figures.

Notice which modality (or modalities) gives you the most ease and also which is the most difficult.

Why does it matter?

We all have a preferred representational system (some of us have more than one) for our conscious thinking. In order to bring something to our conscious awareness, we use a lead representational system. Your lead representational system may be the same as your preferred representational system and it may not.

For example, assume my preferred representational system is visual and my lead representational system is kinaesthetic. If someone asks me about my last holiday, I may first get in touch with all of the good feelings about my trip before fully bringing up the pictures in my mind.

Lead representational systems may vary between contexts.

For example, before accessing the feelings associated with a very distressful event, I may choose to first access the event through pictures and then ease myself into the feelings associated with the event.

Now it's your turn...

Your lead representational system

How about you? Think of a happy time and notice the order or sequence of your own sensory experience and then do the same for a sad time.

So, you're _____ then with _____ secondary and then with _____ following along in third when happy.

But you're _____ then with _____ secondary and then with _____ following along in third when sad.

OK, cool.

This will be really useful information as you continue through the exercises in Part II, when we'll also be accessing that 'happy time' or memory again and putting it to good use.

But what if you are working, living, communicating with someone who is not the same as you?

Sometimes, we just don't speak the same language

Have you ever had the occasion to explain something to someone and they've said, 'I don't *see* what you are saying,' or 'I can't *picture* this.' What's going on here? One possibility is that they are highly visual and you have been using words other than visual references; hence, they are having difficulty forming a *picture* of your explanation in their mind. And how do we usually handle this situation? We repeat the same words over again, only this time LOUDER and SLOWER, as obviously they simply did not hear us!

Given what you know now and creating that flexibility in your own map, how can you approach this differently so the person can *see* what you are saying? Of course, they can't actually *see* what you are saying, but the words you use can help them form a picture in their mind and, of course, that's what we really mean, isn't it?

Well, one possibility is to use visual words to help them make a picture in their mind or alternatively, you may wish to draw them a diagram or an actual picture.

And of course, it is not just visual people who may have difficulty with your explanation. An auditory person may say, 'I can't hear what you are saying,' or 'It doesn't sound right to me.' Well, of course, they can physically *hear what you are saying* and there is nothing wrong with the volume at which you are saying it, but what's making it unclear is that the words you are using are not creating an internal experience that they can make sense of and navigate around. This could simply be because they have no experience or map for it, so we need to help them to find something that they do recognize and then help them to navigate from there.

A kinaesthetic person might say, 'I can't grasp (or get a handle on) what you are saying,' or 'I don't have a feeling for this.' An auditory digital person: 'There is no logic in what you are saying,' or 'This just does not make sense.'

Really pay attention to the words people are using; they are revealing to you how they see, hear, get in touch with or make sense of the world around them and how they construct their map of the world.

Think about this. Have you ever found yourself in what we might call a 'heated agreement' with someone, or is there someone with whom lots of things do fit but for some reason that you can't quite put your finger on – you just don't get along, or you fall out over silly things a lot of the time? You'll have heard yourself complaining that they just don't 'get' you and yet others have no problem, so it can't be your fault, can it? Well, yes and no.

The words you use and hear

The most likely cause for the miscommunication or their not 'getting' you is that you are going from one place (or representational system) and they are rightly coming from theirs; it's just a different place. So while you may well both have the best of intentions, you still manage to fall out a lot of the time. I said you are both right and wrong because, first of all, I want you to think of it as if you are both speaking slightly different languages. Actually, dialects might be a better way to think of it. You recognize and understand most of what they are saying, but some parts are just lost in the fog of translation in your own mind and so you tend to fill in the blanks yourself, making it up in order to make sense of it.

The problem with that, given what we know now, is that you are both already deleting, distorting and generalizing anyway so now you are adding in an element of *making it up* to the *make it fit* so that it makes sense, but you very quickly end up in a place very far from reality. Then, factor in that we understand that thought leads to feeling, meaning that you are generating false feelings and have two people with emotions, too often false emotion talking to false emotion, rather than person to person. When you actually think about it, it's a wonder we ever get anything done and even more of a miracle that the global population continues to grow at such a rate. Let's get back to person to person instead of emotion to emotion, eh?

Then of course, you also get the opposite, where you just *click* with someone. They don't necessarily have to have any of the same normal cultural reference points and, in fact, you don't even have to have the same first language, but for some reason you just click and get on like a house on fire. That is very simply because you both share the same fundamental representation system base so they will *see* your point as you *see* theirs. Or they might *hear what you are saying* while their remarks really *strike a chord* with you or perhaps you are just easily able to *get to grips with it* as they find it easy to *grasp* what you are saying.

Now have a look back at all the words and phrases in italics. What do you notice? They are all very common phrases that we use in everyday speech and life, but do you notice that they are nicely paired: visual-to-visual, auditory-to-auditory and kinaesthetic-to-kinaesthetic? Did you also realize that without thinking about it, the words we use all day, every day tell us so much more than just the information we are trying to convey.

Let me put you in the picture so that you can clearly hear

what I am saying and get a proper handle on this.

No one would ever say that, because in that sentence, we have all three main representational systems well represented. From the visual team, we have *let me put you in the **picture*** representation; for the auditory, we have so you *can clearly **hear** what I am saying* and from the kinaesthetic there is *get a proper **handle** on this.*

Do you ***see*** my point? Sorry, I couldn't resist that.

In the next section, we will really look at how we use language literally and how to use it properly to get what you want, even if that's just from yourself.

Literal language

We all use language really quite literally although you may not have realized it till now. The phrases and figures of speech that we choose (subconsciously), called 'predicates', indicate so much more about us than we think; they also indicate how we think.

As a good NLPer, you will have the flexibility in your own approach to be able to communicate clearly, effectively and even persuasively with anyone, no matter which representation system they (or you) are coming from.

This brings me rather neatly to another phrase we touched on earlier that you will hear a lot in NLP: 'The meaning of communication is the response that you get. This simply means that it is no longer the responsibility of the other person to '*get*' you; it is your responsibility to be *got*. How many times have you heard people deride others because 'they don't understand me'? Well, from now on, it is not their fault; everyone has the capacity to make sense and to make sense of the information they are presented with. So if something doesn't make sense, it can only be because it is not being presented in the correct way.

It's kind of like the difference between 'lecturing' and 'learning'. In lecturing, the information comes out and that's about it; what happens next is up to the student. The responsibility of the lecturer is to inform their audience and that's where it ends; the facts are fired out there and then forgotten about, sadly and all too often, by the audience. I don't know about yours, but that was certainly how my education went. But how different would it (and your life) be if instead the emphasis were on 'learning'? How would it be if the meaning of the communication was the response that the teacher got? How would it be if your teachers were measured on how much learning you did and how much you got, not simply how many hours they spent sending it out there for you to make whatever sense of it you could? The world of education would be an entirely different place, that's for sure!

So from now on, for you and I at least, the meaning of your communication is the response that you get, so if at first someone doesn't get it, try something else. If you are someone who is primarily oriented in a visual sense and they are more auditory, you can begin by trying to include more auditory references in your conversation and *see* how that *resonates* better for them. Give it a shot and notice how you get on.

NLP Know-how

Make sure the conversation is a meaningful one if you want to find some good predicates to work with, because people will not only tell you which their dominant representational system is, but also, if there's a problem, they will very often tell you how to fix it if you listen closely enough and use your new skills. Below you'll find that list again for reference.

Really listen to language literally

How many language predicate references can you spot in the next conversation you have?

VISUAL

Usually memorize by making pictures and less likely to be distracted by noise. Often have trouble remembering audible instructions. They are interested in how something looks and, even if they can remember the sound, they will most likely make a picture of it first.

- See
- Look
- View
- Appear
- Show
- Dawn
- Reveal
- Envision
- Illuminate
- Imagine
- Clear
- Foggy
- Focused
- Hazy
- Crystal
- Picture

AUDITORY

Typically are easily distracted by noise. They can repeat things back to you easily and learn just by listening. They like music and talking on the phone. Tone of voice and the words used are usually very important. You can upset them not by what you say but just by *how* you say it.

- Hear
- Listen
- Sound(s)
- Make music
- Harmonize
- Tune in/out
- Be all ears
- Rings a bell
- Silence
- Be heard
- Resonate
- Deaf
- Mellifluous
- Dissonance
- Question
- Unhearing

KINAESTHETIC

Often speak slowly and *feel* their way. They respond to physical rewards and touching. They memorize things best by doing it, walking through or rehearsing something. They will be interested in a solution that feels right or gives them a good gut feeling.

- Feel
- Touch
- Grasp
- Get hold of
- Slip through
- Catch on
- Tap into
- Make contact
- Throw out
- Turn around
- Hard
- Unfeeling
- Concrete
- Scrape
- Get a handle on
- Solid

AUDITORY DIGITAL

Tend to spend a fair amount of time talking to themselves. Superfluous information annoys them and they memorize by steps, procedures and sequences. They can also sometimes exhibit characteristics of any other representational system.

- Sense
- Experience
- Understand
- Think
- Learn
- Process
- Decide
- Motivate
- Consider
- Change
- Perceive
- Insensitive
- Distinct
- Conceive
- Know

If Chapter One was about paying attention with your eyes, then this chapter has been all about paying attention with your ears. The best NLPers are not the ones who are the slickest with the various techniques, they are the ones who pay most attention and notice most, just as the best doctors are the ones who are really good at diagnosis and not just writing prescriptions. The more you notice, the more choice you have, so it's time to pay real attention, not just to the story but how it is constructed, even if you're the one telling that story.

Chapter 4

From Awareness to Change

We know from earlier that the way we re-present images, sounds and pictures in our minds is what creates our subjective experience of the world around us and that all behaviour is a product of the state of mind you are in at the time. Now, let's explore just how quickly we can change that when we know how. And just how easy it can be to spot where and how to make that change in those around us.

Richard Bandler, the founding creator of NLP, often talks of 'finding the difference that makes the difference' to me. The pictures, sounds, feelings, tastes and smells we re-present on the inside to create our states are a lot like ingredients when we are cooking. They are all variable, but they have to be combined and treated in a certain way to get the same outcome. Let me explain. Say, for example, we were making a chocolate cake. Not being of the culinary persuasion myself, I have taken counsel from my wife, Claire, and having sampled the example (hey, you have to test these things and I am not going to pass anything on to you without testing it myself...) I can tell you that a fairly basic but very tasty chocolate cake usually contains flour, butter, sugar, eggs, vanilla essence and, of course, chocolate!

Obviously, the ingredients must be mixed in the correct quantities and in the correct order and then baked for the desired time at the correct temperature before you can enjoy the fruits of your labours, chocolate cake and a coffee... yum!

Well, it's exactly the same in your head, only in NLP, we call those ingredients 'submodalities' (see page 39–40), which are all the variables we have in the pictures, sounds, feelings, tastes and smells we re-present on the inside.

So if you are predominantly visual, you will make pictures and use visual references naturally in your language, right?

But there is a little more to it than that because, just as with chocolate cake, we have lots of variables to consider if we want to create the optimum cake (and remember that, by cake, we really mean 'state'). Then, within those pictures, sounds, feelings, tastes and smells, we also have lots of subconscious choices about how we do that.

NLP Know-how

Imagine (if you are visual) that the picture you make is big and bright and moving, as though you were seeing a movie on the biggest screen imaginable and in 3D too. Do you think that will be more or less emotive than watching exactly the same movie but on a tiny screen, say, set on the back of the seat in front of us on an aircraft or, worse, viewing a still from the movie in black and white in a newspaper? While the specific content of the image may be the same and the plot line is obviously exactly the same, the whole experience could not be more different.

The same is true for sounds. Contrast the experience of attending a concert or listening to a really good stereo with listening to a crackly old radio or even by just turning the volume down from the level that makes you feel good to a quiet whisper and moving it into the background. Some small changes can change everything... and it is exactly the same in our minds.

So back to our chocolate cake... let's say that we didn't want to make chocolate cake (that 'state') any more. In fact, let's say that for some reason chocolate cake was causing us pain and we wanted to change it. Well, we have some options: we can change any of the submodalities (ingredients), but obviously some of them will have a more profound effect than others. Let's say for example that we first of all took out or turned down the amount of sugar. What would that be like? Well, it would be a lot like the original cake. It would even look exactly the same, but it just wouldn't be quite as sweet when we tasted it. So there's a difference, for sure, but not much of a difference really and certainly not to look at.

Then, let's say that we took out or turned down the chocolate. What would that do? It would make quite a difference this time, more than just taking out the sugar, but we would definitely still have a cake, just not chocolate cake. Let's now say that we took out the flour but left everything else exactly the same, in exactly the same proportions: we mix them in the same way in the same mixing bowl, and we put them in the same oven at the same temperature for the same amount of time. With everything else constant, what do we get? I'm guessing a kind of chocolate-baked omelette, but definitely NOT anything we would recognize as chocolate cake.

And after we baked it like that, could we then go back and add in the flour to return it to cake? No, of course not. The new state is just as permanent as the original version and will serve us well. What we have effectively done is found 'the difference that makes the difference' and changed that. And when you change that, everything else connected to it changes automatically all by itself.

Creating change

So how do you change submodalities to change your subjective experience?

Put simply, anything you can do to a picture, you can do to a picture in your mind's eye. If it's colour, you can make it black and white. If it is moving, you can make it still. If it is big, you can make it small; if you are seeing it through your own eyes, then you can view it from somewhere else. If it is close, you can make it far away. The choice is always there and the choice is always yours.

It's the same with sounds. You can change loud to quiet, a harsh tone to a funny one, your own voice to someone else's, even someone else who makes you laugh, from inside your head to outside your head or from close to far away and many, many more.

Of course, the same is true for feelings, tastes and smells, but we will get to those in just a second.

If all those things are in fact variable and the language we use tells us so much more than just the content, what do you now notice in the following statements?

❖ 'I just need to get some distance on the issue.'

❖ 'I just need some space.'

❖ 'We need to look at the problem from a new perspective.'

First and hopefully, quite obviously, they all use visual language, but second (for bonus points), did you notice that not only is the *distance*, *space* or *perspective* significant, but we are also being told exactly what needs to happen in order to make us feel better.

Case study

One of my very first and still very fastest pieces of change work ever happened when I worked with a woman who was 'stressed to the max' (her words) and after about 30 seconds said, 'I just need to get some distance on the issue.'

I asked, 'Why, where is it now?'

'It feels like it's right here,' she said, and held her hand about two inches from her face.

As quick as you like I got up, walked across to her and moved her hand out to arm's length, 'How's that'? I asked.

'Wow,' she said, 'that is so much better already.'

Simple as that! Now calmer, we then continued our session to help resolve her stress.

What we will almost certainly find is that if we close our eyes and think about the problem, the image that comes to mind will be very close, too close, in fact, and in being too close, it feels oppressive and uncomfortable. Doesn't it just seem rather obvious that if something is uncomfortably close, moving it further away will immediately feel better? Well, it does to me...

Perhaps that's why NLP felt so intuitive when I was a learner just like you. So what about the phrase, 'we need to look at the problem from a new perspective' – what does that tell you? Well, it's a bit like when you might hear a journalist ask, 'What's the angle on the story,' and, in fact, it's a lot like you experience yourself when you go to the cinema. For now, just forget about the movie itself and imagine that you walk into a completely empty movie theatre and you can sit anywhere you want. Where do you sit? I would be about halfway back and on the right-hand side as I looked at the screen. What about you? We all have our preference and for the most part, we assume that it's just one of those things. It's not, in the cinema, we are orienting ourselves relative to the screen for best effect.

As we delve deeper into the workings of the mind and our experience, we learn that it is never 'just one of those things'. Everything we do, we do for a reason. All our actions are the result of a meta program that we are running in our head that guides us in everything we do: from the way we walk and talk to the way we react in situations to the way we feel and even where we prefer to sit in the movies. If the phrase 'we need to look at the problem from a new perspective' tells us anything, it's that the person saying it wants to look at things from another place and a new 'angle'. Or perhaps, you'll also hear them say that they are a 'big picture person'. All these little figures of speech tell us so much about how someone is orienting things on the inside in order for them to make best 'sense' of it. At the movies, we can't move the screen to suit ourselves but we can certainly move ourselves in relation to the screen.

NLP Know-how

As a slight aside, on the first day of school, all the children file into class and choose where they want to sit... for no particular reason, just randomly or so it seems. Most often, visual people tend to sit near the window, the big picture people sit at the back and the detail guys and girls at the front; the creatives on the left and the more logical ones on the right. That's just how it works. Then the teacher wonders why the students by the window are always staring out of it daydreaming. Well, unless what's in the room in front of them is bigger and brighter and bolder and more engaging than what they can see out of the window, what's out there will always get their attention. And if it isn't, they will make up their own pictures and internal reality anyway.

So, where's your favourite place to sit in the movies or in a classroom? Now imagine sitting in exactly the opposite location. If you're a back and right person, then imagine sitting in the front left – how does it feel? It feels weird, right? Nothing has happened any differently in the 'real' world – the movie hasn't even played yet – but just sitting there feels a bit odd. Well, that's because we orient pictures in the way that makes most sense to us and if the picture is coming from the *wrong* place, it just doesn't feel quite right.

Listen for visual references

From now on, listen very carefully for visual references in conversations you have (especially when you are not the one speaking) and notice when the person (even if it's you) is setting out exactly what's happening and how to make it better.

But what if you don't hear many visual references? What if the person tends to be much more auditory? I'm sure you've heard people say things like, 'If I could just stop this nagging doubt' or 'I'm worried sick'. You'll have heard those expressions and more, I'm sure. 'I hear you loud and clear' or to 'tune in' to what someone is saying or even 'unheard of' (look again at the checklist on page 55) are all examples of auditory language being used to *clearly illustrate* (to use a visual reference) that the person is constructing their subjective experience primarily in an auditory sense.

So what do you think we do if 'I just need to quiet my thinking'? What is the problem? Well, we all have much more control than we perhaps think we do and so, if you were to ask the person to close their eyes and 'tune in' to what happens inside of them when they think about the situation, you will most likely find that their thoughts are too loud. You can play with this for yourself right now, too. Have you ever had the experience of listening to the radio or TV and the volume is just one little increment higher than you would ideally have it? It's just not right, is it? And also, just how annoying is it? To illustrate my point, close your own eyes and think a nice relaxing thought. How about simply 'relax, relax, relax...'? Now as you do that notice how it feels in your body. Then I want you progressively to turn up your own internal volume until you are shouting 'RELAX, RELAX, RELAX' to yourself in your mind. How does that feel now? Anything but relaxing, isn't it?

So with the person's eyes closed, or yours if it's you (just so that they are not distracted and can focus exclusively on the inside without the outside world getting in the way), ask them to rate how they feel on a scale from

1 to 10, with 10 being most annoyed and 1 being fine and calm. Then, ask them to rate the volume of their 'thoughts' on that same scale, with 10 being blaringly loud and 1 being no more than a whisper. Now, ask them to turn down the volume on their thoughts just like you would turn it down on the TV or on the radio.

I am very fortunate to have worked with many different people in my career. It has even been said that perhaps I have done more one-to-one sessions than anyone else working in NLP today but, that aside, one particularly auditory client comes to mind.

Case study

The condition was severe; the result was profound, but the solution was remarkably simple. We'll call my client Dan (because that was his name). Dan had only ever eaten five different foods: chips, bread and butter, tomato soup (strained), pizza (but only cheese and tomato pizza) and custard. He was about 18 when he came to see me because he was finding it increasingly difficult to have a 'normal' life with such a restrictive diet – not to mention the rather obvious health implications. So Dan came and sat in my chair and we got chatting about stuff... random stuff, mainly golf, which he loved to play and, as it turned out, was rather good at.

It would all have appeared very conversational to the untrained eye or ear but, of course, it was to establish his dominant representation system and how he constructed his subjective experiences. He turned out to be very auditory with kinaesthetic and then a little visual.

I began by asking him what his worst food memory was. Immediately he said, 'Oh, that's easy; it was a Chinese buffet. We had gone as a family to see a Christmas show and stopped for some food on the way. It was definitely my idea of hell.'

That's quite typical in my experience. People can almost always remember the first, the worst and the most recent experience with whatever it is that they are scared of. 'So what happened?' I asked. 'Not what happened in the restaurant, that's not particularly relevant to how to change it, what happened in your head?'

For a moment, Dan looked down, thinking, and then from side to side as though checking in with something and said, 'Well, this might sound daft, but when I see a food that's not on my safe list, it's like a little voice in my head just says, "no, no, don't do it" and then I just get scared and back away or go straight to one of the things I know I am OK with.' (As he spoke, Dan pointed to the left side of his head with his left hand and to his solar plexus with his right, not directly but so casually that you'd never have thought anything of it. After all, people move their hands all the time and it doesn't mean anything, does it?) 'That day, I remember just having chips. I remember the disappointment on my mum's face and also feeling really disappointed in myself. Part of me really wanted to try but I just couldn't bring myself to do it.'

Plenty to work with there, *I thought, but the most obvious thing was the voice in his head. Now, Dan clearly wasn't really 'hearing voices', he just meant his thoughts, that little voice we all have in our heads – it's us talking to ourselves – and Dan's internal dialogue was telling him what to do; he was doing just that and scaring himself witless in the process.*

Two things we need to know here are, first, no matter what the pattern or the behaviour, your brain is not trying to hurt you; even a severely phobic response like Dan's had a very strong positive intention. In his case, the intention was to keep him safe from the perceived threat or the danger of trying something new. Second, obviously we are not going to be able to change all the food in the world so we're back to changing the subjective experience of it, as always.

Just like with the experience of the movie being much less on a small screen than it would be at the cinema, I wondered how loud the 'voice' was in his head and what the tone of voice was like. 'Oh, it's loud,' he said, 'deafening in fact, and in a really harsh, almost panicky tone.' (Try the exercise, 'Turning down your internal volume', on page 71 and you can experience this for yourself now.)

When he thought about the situation, even years later, it still caused him that same feeling of panic and fear. 'Turn the volume on the thoughts down, all the way down,' I said, 'and then move the sound so that it's right outside your head, like it's on a speaker that's getting further away.'

As he did that and, in about ten seconds flat, his shoulders dropped, his face relaxed and without any prompting from me, he let out a sigh and said, 'Wow, it's gone.'

'What's gone?' I asked.

'The feeling; I can still think of the situation, I can remember it, but that horrible panic feeling in my chest has just gone.'

Change happens fast, and in my experience, it always happens fast when you get it right like this, but I wasn't finished there...

He had told us that earlier when he said, 'Part of me really wanted to try, but I just couldn't bring myself to do it.' And now I wanted to take his natural curiosity and get it working for him, for a change, so I asked him, 'You know before you went to the restaurant and you were curious about what other food might be like? What was that curiosity like; how did you know you were curious?'

This time, he pointed to the right side of his head with one hand and again to his chest with the other, a little higher up this time, if you cared to notice. This time, I wanted him to be navigating more by the feelings than thoughts and so I simply asked him to give the feeling in his chest a colour, a shape, a size and even a texture, all of which he did easily, and then said, 'Take the feeling and double it in size.' As his curiosity grew and grew, I anchored that kinaesthetically by touching his shoulder with my hand and after just a few seconds, asked him to open his eyes and come back out. We'll get to the technique of anchoring later, but for now all you need to know is that timing is everything and as Dan's curiosity grew and I anchored it, I released the anchor and opened his eyes just as he approached what I calibrated was close to peak state.

When I asked him to close his eyes and try to get the memory back, would you believe that he couldn't? All he could feel was a sense of curiosity and the longer he stayed with it, the more it grew inside him.

Knowing that this memory had been the worst, we then repeated the pattern from the first or, in fact, the first that he could remember, as this problem had existed since he was about two years old. I later learned from his mum that he had never really made the transition to solids. In the absence of making up any stories about that and just sticking to what was there, we fixed them one by one, the worst, then the first and then the most recent.

It was a couple of days before I heard from Dan again; I think it was the day that he discovered ice cream. That day will go down in history as one of the best of his life, I think, but he also told me what happened the day he left me. He met his gran who had brought him to Glasgow and they went to a nearby café. Without even thinking, Dan ordered a sandwich and a coffee – no big deal you might think, but unheard of for him. His gran then sat and watched as he finished those before working his way through most of the options on the cake counter and then asked what was for dinner.

In all, the session took about 45 minutes. The difference that made all the difference was that when he didn't have the thought in his head, or he couldn't get it, then the feeling just never came and when that happened, he allowed himself to go back home to his own inner wellbeing and curiosity that had been there all the time.

NLP Know-how

Remember, with the principle of primacy (the first) and regency (the most recent) and then taking the worst and knowing that patterns of three always tend to work best in the subconscious mind. For example, you might remember Tony Blair's speech in which he repeated 'Education, education, education' to fully embed his point at a party conference prior to being elected in 1997. Or, going back further into the history of great orators, Margaret Thatcher's famous 'No, no, no' speech. The pattern of triple repetition really helps to embed or break habits in the mind. So if something is worth saying, it's worth repeating. Repetition is key and three times is king... so if it's worth saying it's worth repeating, got it?

Repetition is key

What you will find with an auditory person is that the volume is almost directly proportional to their state, but just like with you and the TV volume, if it's even only one increment too loud, they will have a tipping point. And when their internal volume is lower than their auditory threshold, they will almost automatically relax back into feeling OK.

Turning down your internal volume

Just try it quickly. Close your eyes if it's safe to do so. If it's not, then put the book down too and concentrate! And just take any phrase you want, 'Mind the gap', for instance, but say it REALLY LOUDLY and in a panicked tone of voice to yourself over and over again. How does that feel?

It feels a bit frightening, doesn't it? Well, if that's just you making something up, it should be clear the effect it has in the 'real' world. Now, just for fun, think of another phrase, maybe one that you often use yourself, but do it in the same loud, anxious voice. It feels much the same, right? That's because the *content* doesn't really matter that much. Only 7 per cent of all communication is the words we use; everything else, 93 per cent, is how we use them.

When we use NLP therapeutically, one of the great benefits is that we don't have to go back into the story and dig up all those old painful memories in order to try to make it better; it's just not necessary. The story doesn't matter that much anyway; as we already know, it is only ever at very most an approximation of what happened and, as we also know, it changes every time we access it. So I'm sure that you, like me, will find it difficult to understand how continually opening up old wounds just so you can talk about it and put labels on it could actually help make it go away. It just seems obvious that if you have a big, bright, bold, scary image in your mind's eye or your internal dialogue is screaming at you and every time it's triggered (consciously or subconsciously), you feel the feelings that go with it, then all you have to do to feel better is to stop making those big scary pictures or turn the volume down or change the tone.

You can even make the same picture or the same words, but if it's small and black and white or squeaky, funny and insignificant, that's exactly how it will feel. Easier said than done though, eh? Well, actually no... easier done than said; that's why I want you to use this book to guide you and practise, practise, practise. Repetition is the key here and you just need to get familiar with listening to language literally and knowing what to do.

So we know what to look and listen out for, but what about that third dominant set of submodalities, feelings? Before we go into exploring our feelings and how to change them, it is important to remember the relationship between thought and feeling and then between feeling, action and outcome.

Thoughts lead to feelings, plain and simple. We make pictures and sounds in our heads; we generally call those thoughts, which automatically create feelings in our bodies. The problem for most of us is that we're not actually aware of the thoughts but are very much aware of the feelings.

Feelings: They're on the move.

Feelings only tend to be noticed when they move; think about that and even about how we tend to describe our feelings. Most often, we use some kind of moving adjective, which is then associated with the precise area in the body where the feeling sits. For example, look at the following often-used phrases:

❖ 'My head was *spinning*.'

❖ 'My stomach *churned*.'

- ❖ 'My heart *sank.*'

- ❖ 'I was *down* in the dumps.'

- ❖ 'I was as *high* as a kite.'

In fact, lots of the time when we describe our emotions, we ascribe a sense of movement or direction to them.

Case study

I'll tell you about one of my extreme vertigo clients and let's pay particular attention to the feelings. We have already said that feelings are only feelings when they move, but have you ever noticed which way *they move? I was working with a client the other day who had a terrible fear of heights, so much so that she couldn't even stand on a chair to change a light bulb. Even when she stood on something less than a metre high, she would get this feeling that rushed up and forwards and it felt like she was going to fall off, almost like she was being pulled forwards. In fact, the* Oxford English Dictionary's *definition of vertigo is 'a sensation of whirling and loss of balance, associated particularly with looking down from a great height'.*

'A sensation of whirling...' So it even 'officially' has a sense of movement to it and when my client stood on a chair, that sensation of whirling whirled up and forwards and tried to pull her over so she felt like she was going to fall. Because she felt like she was going to fall, her brain kicked in and created the rush of adrenaline, which we call 'fear', in order to make sure she protected herself. Even though she was only a little

way off the ground, the positive intention was clear; it was just turned up way too high.

So if up and forwards felt like it was pulling her over the edge, what do you think changing it to back and down would feel like? Well, I wondered too, so that's what I did. I got her to give the feeling a colour, a texture and to rate it on a scale of 1 to 10 as to how it made her feel and then to move that feeling outside. I counted down from 3 to 1 and then asked her to put the feeling in reverse, so that instead of it going up and forwards, it went back and down and round and round like that. Then I asked her to take the feeling back inside herself and keep it going back and down and back and down. Her shoulders dropped, she gave a sigh and said that it felt immediately and completely different. I then asked her to keep the feeling going like that and to step up onto my chair, no problem at all, and again all in a matter of minutes.

Small change, big difference

I am always looking for the seemingly small change that makes a really big difference. Just like removing the flour from a cake recipe. No matter what else you have, if you don't have flour then you can't make a cake; if you change the key submodality then you can't construct the state either. NLP is a vast and varied subject but the fundamentals are very simple.

Remember, in order to be anything other than OK, we must be doing something to take ourselves away from our own wellbeing.

For people with vertigo, it is not really a fear of heights that's the problem. It's that when they are up high, they have a feeling in their bodies that's pulling them up and forwards and it feels like they are being pulled over the edge. It is that fear of falling or being pulled over the edge that is the problem. We are only hard-wired to be afraid of two things – falling and sudden loud noises – everything else is learned. So it's not a fear of heights that's the problem; it's a fear of falling due to the sensation of being pulled towards or over the edge. But when you take that same feeling that is 'whirling' up and forwards in the body and spin it backwards, so that it goes back and down (everyone has the ability to do this; we just don't realize it), then the feeling completely changes and not only goes away, but you actually feel more anchored, grounded and safe. And just as with all these examples, nothing whatsoever has changed in the 'real' world!

Now, think of the term *depression*. Which way does depression go? Even just thinking about the word tends to pull you down that way, doesn't it? It does for me and I just don't understand why you would label something with a title that actually makes it worse. How depressed do you think people would feel if it were called something much more *uplifting*?

To me, depression is just anger or frustration without the enthusiasm. But try telling that to someone who has been diagnosed with 'it' and I'm not sure they'd see the funny side... if you get my point. But have you noticed how we are encouraged to talk about things like depression as if they are something that we catch or that just kind of happen *to* us? 'Oh no, I caught a dose of the depression; maybe it was from a door handle. How careless is it that all those depressed people are spreading it around the place.'

You may well laugh now, but depression is really no laughing matter. And with the number of prescriptions for antidepressants increasing exponentially every year, it would appear that never in the history of mankind has the world been more depressed. How can that be? Very few of us are in physical danger every day. Very few of us wonder where the next meal is coming from and, for the most part, we have shelter, security and friendship. So if all our basic needs are met, so why is it that we are so damn depressed?

Well, what we know, of course, is that in order to feel depression or any other feeling for that matter, we must first do something in our heads to create that feeling. So, what is it that people do to make themselves disappointed or even depressed? Simple, they go inside and tell themselves stories in glorious technicolour about how things don't measure up to their expectations.

When polled, the vast majority of people saying they were 'depressed' cited that their life was a bit of a disappointment compared to what they hoped/expected it to be. Richard Bandler has a great line, which is that 'disappointment takes adequate planning', meaning that in order to be disappointed, we must have a preconceived idea of what something is going to be like to which the reality fails to match up.

Think about another simple turn of phrase that we use when shopping: 'I just can't find what I am looking for.' If we read that literally as it's intended, we can clearly see that in order not to be able to find what we are looking for, then we simply must have an idea of what that is. You will also have found yourself browsing similar items before exclaiming, 'It's just not quite right.' It doesn't matter what we are shopping for, from black shoes for work to a new house, we go searching for what we are *looking* for. We try to match the reality of the outside with the constructed image on the inside, and when they don't match up, or match closely enough, then we feel the feeling of being disappointed.

So if 'disappointment takes adequate planning' and we know that we need to *do* something in order to feel anything other than our default setting (which is OK), then might it be an idea to stop doing it? And do you think that in stopping doing it, we would feel better? Yes, of course, and that part is, in fact, automatic.

But for the most part, we don't get that and so start from the premise that there is something wrong with us. The fastest way to feel bad is to compare yourself to someone else. In other words, compare what you know about yourself with what you think about someone else. We've all done it; please stop now.

You will automatically reset back to happy much, much faster than you think as soon as you lose your attachment to believing the thoughts in your head.

Just because you think it does not make it true

In fact, the feelings you feel are much more to do with the way you construct those thoughts than they are to do with the thoughts themselves. You can and will automatically go back to being OK as soon as you break the attachment to the expectation.

I say automatic because our default setting is happy. In fact, if you are striving to be happy, you are definitely doing it the wrong way round. It's a bit like *trying* to relax; how do you even do that?

Just as the nature of water is clear, the nature of we humans is to be OK and happy, and so much of what you will learn in this book is effectively ways to press the reset button and allow yourself to go back to OK. For that reason, there will be no *maintenance*, nothing to remember to do and absolutely nothing to *keep up*. You will simply go back to being OK because, in the absence of anything pulling you out of shape, that's what happens; you go back to being OK, just like that.

You'll hear me talk a lot about 'pressing the reset button' because, for me, that's what this is all about. Now I know there are lots of people who will talk about using NLP to create 'optimum state' or ' building a resourceful state', but for me, there is nothing more 'optimum' and 'resourceful' than putting people back to their natural default setting, which is to be OK. When we stay out of our own way for long enough, we tend to do just great.

Think about that for a second. Who and how would you be if you weren't caught up in the thoughts in your head and feeling the feelings that go with them? Well, you'd still be you, right? But I'm guessing you'd be a very much better, calmer, more creative, loving, joyful version of you. And all you have to do is let go.

Play with your submodalities

As a simple guide, anything you can do to a picture you can do to a picture in your mind's eye. Anything you can do to sound you can do to internal sound, while feelings are generally only noticed when they move or have a sense of size and shape.

Just play with it for now... Close your eyes and think of the good memory from before (*see exercise on page 48*). You can even refer back to the 'submodalities checklist' too (*see page 39*). Now play it... think of it as a TV that you have complete control over.

If the picture is colour make it black and white, if it's moving make it still, if it's big make it small... I'm sure you get the idea. Notice the difference to how making these changes makes you feel.

Put it back the way it was before, now.

Do the same for any sounds in the memory. If the sound is loud make it quiet, if it's a harsh tone make it soft or even funny. If the sound is inside your head, push it far away. Just go through all the entries in your submodalities checklist and change what you can and notice the difference, and the difference that makes the most difference.

Finally it's time to pay attention to your feelings. Close your eyes and access that memory again. Now this time pay attention to where the feeling is in your body. Think of your feeling as an object; what size, shape, colour, texture does it have? Which direction does it move in? Again anything you can do to an object you can do to the feeling. Change the size, shape, colour, texture, direction it's moving one at a time and notice the difference it makes to how you feel... cool eh?

In Part II, we are going to get more into the techniques of NLP. But now that we have the foundations, I'm sure you can already see just how quickly things can slot into place when you listen properly to what people say and listen to their language literally for a change, because when you do that, you can really begin to get a handle on how we construct our subjective experience and understand what makes us tick. Just remember that we are all different, but we all construct our internal reality using the same building blocks of pictures, sounds, feelings, tastes and smells, and that the story doesn't matter when you make the screen smaller and the lyrics don't affect you if you can't hear them and that feelings are only really feelings when they move, but you can change that. Then you know that while the world may well be fixed and solid, how we feel about it is open to change from any minute to the next and that change happens fast, always.

So now that you know that we all construct our own internal states, please stop every time you notice yourself say, 'I think' when you don't have any real evidence; stop and know that you are really only taking a reality check from your own imagination. How useful do you think that is?

Part II

THE TECHNIQUES OF NLP

'In Neuro-Linguistic Programming, we don't "treat" patients; we give people lessons on how to think and make better choices.'
RICHARD BANDLER, *GUIDE TO TRANCE-FORMATIONS*

Chapter 5

Matching, Mirroring, Pacing, Leading and... Commanding!

I'm sure you'll have had the experience of meeting a person for the first time and knowing instantly that this is the sort of person you can do business or be friends with. Everything you say or do seems to click and you just feel pleased to know the other person. You may have walked away afterwards and said something like, 'We got on like a house on fire from the first words we spoke.' Or even, 'It was love at first sight.' Clearly rapport is a feeling and a visual if you really want to break it down like that.

There are countless instances in our private and business lives where we need to begin creating rapport with another person. It can be so useful to become skilled at rapport building. Get good at it and it'll stand you in very good stead in all areas of your life with other people.

Perhaps you are attending a job interview like our candidate earlier (*see page 21*), hoping to make a sale to a customer or wishing to create a great first impression with the guy or girl of your dreams. All great examples of rapport situations and we have all had that experience of just having *clicked* with someone and feeling that we really liked them and vice versa without truly knowing them that well.

How about at a party with strangers? Have you ever found yourself feeling more at ease with some than others, even though you don't know any of them at all well? Almost as if you have nothing to base it on, nothing you can put your finger on, and yet there's definitely something there.

You have, I know, also had the completely opposite experience. It seems as if you are talking to a brick wall. The other person seems to have perhaps just a flicker, or no interest at all, in what you are saying. Even if you stood there all day, you are convinced that you would make no progress and you'd do as well talking to a lamppost.

We think of people as easy or difficult to get along with, but it is much more likely that we just haven't taken the time or trouble to communicate with each other properly. We have all been there, and it could happen again, but now it doesn't have to.

Why do we need to create rapport?

Being able to build great rapport with another person is a powerful skill to have when used ecologically/honestly. It allows you to connect with another person so they trust you much more and at a different level – here are some examples of when building deep and meaningful rapport is a great thing to do:

❖ For anyone that works as a coach – being in rapport with your client allows them to feel at ease; you'll get a better result for the client as they hold less back.

❖ Anyone that works in education – if a student trusts you, they will learn better and faster.

❖ Those in the medical profession – patients tend to open up more to professionals they trust; often, patients can be nervous or anxious so if that patient trusts you, it allows you to deliver a more relaxed and quality service.

❖ Anyone who works in customer service or sales or in fact anyone dealing with people or who helps anyone else in any way.

There are so many other examples, but what do you notice about the ones above?

The **other** person always has a better experience because of it!

There are many ways to build rapport – most work best when you practise the techniques so that you are able to do them unconsciously without even thinking.

❖ **Match your client's breathing:** This automatically brings your physiologies into alignment with one another. As they breathe in and out, just match your breathing to theirs.

NLP Know-how

If you are talking to a woman, it's probably not appropriate to look at her chest going up and down – you have to be in pretty great rapport already for that. But often you just can't see a person's breathing anyway. So when she is talking, breathe out while she speaks, and breathe in when she stops. It is impossible to speak without breathing out (try it) so this way you'll be perfectly in time every time.

❖ **Match their body movements**: If they have their legs crossed, do the same. Or perhaps (and a little subtler), cross another part of your body. If they lean forwards, match that movement too... subtly though or they will just think you're a bit odd.

❖ **Reflect their choice of words back to them:** If they use visual words (see, looks, visualize, etc.) then use this language too – it may feel a little awkward but it will allow you to build rapport faster and deeper, and unless you are really clumsy, they will never notice.

You know the difference between theory and practice... in theory, everything works, but in practice, you have to work at it.

Building rapport

The next time you are in a meeting or social situation with lots of other people and it's all going well, just take a look around the room. I bet that the majority of the people's body language will be in synch: they'll all cross their legs together or lean back in their chairs at the same time. If you pay particular attention, they will be more or less breathing at the same rate too. This is true rapport in action.

If you then deliberately mismatch these actions, you'll feel your body stepping out of rapport. You may even notice other people looking round at you and a shift in the energy in the room. Try it, it's odd but it works... then, when you are one-to-one with someone and you are in rapport, deliberately move in your chair, take a drink of coffee or cross your legs and notice what happens. If you are in good robust rapport, they will do something very similar within a second or two.

NLP Know-how

If you are in sales, do not ask for the order until you can make them drink or cross or uncross their legs. If you can't do that, then you still have work to do!

This really is a powerful technique; use it wisely and carefully.

Breaking rapport

I know this might sound counterintuitive, especially in a chapter about building rapport, but it is incredibly useful to break rapport (even if you don't really mean it) when you are trying to get your own way.

I need to state right up front that I never ever do this with those closest to me because I am just not inclined that way. I know people who do, but for me this strays a little too far into manipulation territory for my liking. However, I know many people who use this technique to great effect in everyday life. My job here is to teach you the technique; how you use it – well, that's up to you.

But be honest now, have you ever temporarily withheld a hug or a kiss from your partner or been just a little bit standoffish so that they will come to you for one instead? OK, think about it another way: if you have ever worked in a service job, you will know exactly what I mean here. Let's say it's a restaurant and all the diners are enjoying having a casual lunch. You have been chatting to some of them and the other staff and it's all very comfortable and friendly, but there is one customer about whom, although they were polite when they came in and they have not complained, you have the feeling that they just might. Nothing is really wrong, but something you can't quite put your finger on lets you know that it's not quite right either. I'm sure you know what I mean.

Now I'm not saying that in a restaurant, everyone is in perfectly matched and mirrored rapport, but this person really is not and it shows – so whom do you make the most effort to please? It's this customer, isn't it? Whether you like it or not, you do and that's how most people feel when another person is out of rapport with them.

In general, as humans, we like to be liked and for people to be pleased with us and we like/need/crave the social feedback so will go out of our way to get it

Mismatching

Breaking rapport state, or what NLP calls 'mismatching', and triggering that desire in the other person to come to you can be a very, very effective tactic when influencing conversations. And breaking rapport doesn't have to be by becoming sullen and quiet and withholding affection. Remember only 7 per cent of all communication is the words we use; everything else is non-verbal and you can subtly break rapport in many different ways. Note – you do need to be in rapport to begin with.

Perhaps you need to move away or just break eye contact. The way you move your eyes is often a very good way to break rapport. You may even need to avert your eyes altogether.

You may instead change the tone of your voice. A sudden deepening of the voice may change the whole character of a conversation.

When in rapport notice the next time the other person moves, but this time, resist the urge to do the same. They move, you don't and the rapport on that level is broken. Wait a little while and then you move and see what they do; if they move 'on command' from you, then they are trying to earn their way back into rapport and you now have the upper hand, so to speak.

Again, practising breaking rapport is a skill worth cultivating because there are many situations when you will need to be able to do it very subtly without causing offence.

Once you have established some sort of rapport with the person, you are then in pole position to take control of the situation and move in a direction of your choosing as you see fit, ethically, of course.

Pacing and leading

Try these two quick pacing-and-leading techniques and see how quickly you can get that other person to follow your lead.

Technique 1. A subtler take on mirroring

Just like with mirroring body language (*see page 86*), if the person you're talking to likes to start a conversation by getting out a pen and turning to a new page, even though they never write anything down, you might want to copy that gesture as well (but do it very subtly). If that person speaks in a soft tone of voice, then soften your voice as well. If they cross their legs, you cross some part of your body, your arms perhaps. If they tap their foot when their leg is crossed, then you move your finger. Here, you are mirroring the 'form' that they are taking. Get that right and then move on to technique 2, where we will be working with the words they use.

Technique 2: Restating facts and then taking control

This is so straightforward and involves simply stating something true about the person you're talking to – or the situation you're dealing with – and getting the person to agree with you (verbally or not) before you set up to take control.

For example, if you want to convince somebody to donate to a good cause, begin by telling the person something factual like, 'You're here in this restaurant, listening to me talk about raising money for my cancer charity' and then implanting new thoughts by adding, 'and perhaps you're beginning to wonder why should you want to donate to this cause...' Insert what you will after that phrase and I'm sure you can take it from there. There is also another sneaky little NLP hypnotic pattern at play here that we will come to shortly, but for now I'll just flag it up to you as an 'embedded command'.

In this interaction, when you have built rapport and then paced to something that is definitely true, they are in 'this restaurant' and they are 'listening to you talk', but then you have led them in the direction of thinking about them 'donating' and, if you pay close attention to the precise language, you have gone even further than that. You have actually told them or embedded the command 'you want to donate to this cause...' Alternatively the following could be just as good, 'Perhaps you are beginning to wonder how *donating to this cause is a good idea.*' I'm sure you see how this works and we will explore it fully next, but for now I'll let you *just become really curious* about how *it works* and how *it works for you.*

If you've tried out those two techniques, you'll have seen how easy the rapport and pacing-and-leading techniques are? You can use them on virtually anyone and for any situation although another skilled NLPer will quickly spot what you are up to for everyday practice; why don't you test them out on someone who doesn't know anything about NLP, someone whose behaviour you might want to change a little?

For example, if your boss has a tendency to talk too quickly and it makes you feel uneasy and defensive, you can easily use the first technique to control their speed of speech. When they talk to you, answer them back at the same speed to build rapport. Do this three or four times before gradually slowing down your own speech. Do it incrementally and notice if they are following along, so long as you maintain rapport, and you can use your other skills to do this while adjusting the speed. Then your boss will just keep following your lead.

NLP pacing and leading is perhaps one of the easiest techniques to play with. Anyone can do it and in any situation where they are with another person. But, as I said right at the start of the section, now that you know how to manipulate situations accordingly, I trust that you'll use this knowledge positively and only ever ethically and for the greater good, not just for your own benefit. Use it to improve your own communication and persuasion skills but definitely help others as well!

Embedded commands

Before properly getting to grips with embedded commands, often seen as the Holy Grail of persuasion, first it's important to know that how you deliver the words and patterns you are about to learn is absolutely key to making any of this work successfully and not just making yourself look a little silly. But before we get to the embedded commands themselves, I need to teach you the 'bed' into which they are placed.

Embedded commands involve indirectly making suggestions within a larger statement by making a distinction, usually with your voice lower, slower or louder, but they can also take the form of a pause or noise or break of rapport for a split second before the command is delivered.

In NLP, we call this 'marking out' of the command an analogue mark. Analogue communication is a language technique or pattern that is often used during hypnosis to help the subject to take in the commands, bypassing the logical conscious mind. It confuses the logical expectation of the conscious mind and thus allows direct access to the unconscious mind, which is where real change takes place. You embed the commands in the way that you deliver them and by non-verbally marking out some portion of a communication, the unconscious mind identifies and understands this part differently. It signals, 'Pay particular attention to this bit.'

This marking-out can be solely behavioural, such as a body language, gesture or movement or looking away and then back or using voice tone, volume and speed to make that part of the sentence stand out from the rest. Here follow a few examples for you.

❖ 'My friend knows how to *feel really good* about herself.' Here saying the phrase in italics slightly louder, slower or faster than the rest of the sentence can emphasize the 'feel really good'.

❖ 'There is no need to *relax now and go into a trance* just yet.' 'Relax now and go into a trance' could be marked with a hand gesture, or a pause just before the word 'relax'.

❖ 'You can *talk to me* when you are ready.' 'Talk to me' could be marked with a body movement.

Or perhaps in the classroom:

❖ 'John, *sit down and relax*.' 'Sit down and relax' is marked out as a command.

The difference in delivery between a question and a command

The clue may very well be in the title, but you really do need to make sure you deliver the command part of the sentence as a definite command and in language, we understand a rising tone at the end of a sentence as a question and a downward inflection to be a command. There is a difference between 'You are going now?' and 'You are going now.'

Or even...

❖ '*You* are going now.'

❖ 'You *are* going now.'

❖ 'You are *going*, now.'

❖ 'You are going *now*.'

Have you ever noticed how some people seem to be questioning when they don't mean to? 'I *will* get this done by close of play?' But with a rising inflection that can make someone seem hesitant, as if they are asking permission even when the words (only 7 per cent, remember) say exactly the opposite. So, just remember when practising embedded commands:

❖ A question has a rising tone or inflection at the end.

❖ A statement has no inflection at the end.

❖ A command has a downward inflection at the end.

The secret to this chapter is practise, practise, practise. It's time to take your new skills on the road. My top tip is to practise with people you don't know, especially with people who don't know you're 'doing it'. People's behaviour can change dramatically when they become conscious that you might be watching them closely. If they notice, or appear to clam up, then you need to stop and just try again somewhere else. Stealth is the name of the game.

Chapter 6

It's Time for a Change

In NLP the term 'timeline' is used to describe the way that we internally represent time and space to and within ourselves. We each represent the past, present and future differently. But our ability to determine whether an event has happened in the past, is happening in the present or is a future projection comes by matching the experience to our unique internal timeline.

Let me show you. Close your eyes if it's safe to do so and point to your future. Notice exactly where you are pointing. Now, point to the past, which will usually be in exactly the opposite direction to the future, which kind of make sense, doesn't it? Now look at the diagram below...

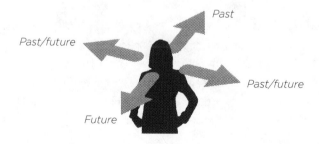

While, of course, it is possible for your timeline to be a virtual line through time and space in almost any direction, the most common versions are for the future to be out in front and the past to be behind. Or, perhaps, the future pointing slightly up or slightly down. In some cases, the future might go straight up and the past straight down or even across in front from left to right or right to left, but this is quite unusual.

However, the diagram on the previous page shows how we generally orient time against space with the past as being directly behind, the future directly in front and to either side, whilst there are varying degrees of the past moving into the future and the future back into the past. That said, everyone's timeline is unique and, as with most things in NLP, it's best to try it out and see in which direction your future lies, and your past too, for that matter. Use the diagram above to help you, but remember your past may not feel as though it's exactly behind you and your future may not feel as though it's exactly in front – as the diagram shows, they can be off to either side too, and to varying degrees; your timeline is completely personal to you.

To help you to understand this and embed things a bit more, here are some simple steps to identify your own timeline.

NLP Know-how

A word of caution: taking yourself or another person into their past using a timeline can cause the release of a tremendous amount of emotion. This is usually a good thing – however, it's important to know what you're doing and if in doubt enlist the help of an experienced NLPer when working with someone other than yourself.

To that end, you must already have built good, strong, robust rapport and, much more importantly, need to be coming from the right place in yourself and with positive intentions too. Of course, that goes for everything you do when working with someone else, but is definitely worth emphasizing here.

When it comes to the opposite, taking someone to explore and rehearse their future, the outcome is almost always beneficial. But it is still important that you always move the other person forwards in any challenges or issues, so that they are left in a positive state.

Visual timeline: The technique

Sit comfortably, close your eyes and imagine seeing your timeline stretching out in front of you and a goal somewhere in your future. You're just practising right now so make sure it's something in the mid-to close distance. In other words something that is not too far off into the future. As you're practising, nothing too major either, because you are just finding your feet, so no higher that a 7/10. Perhaps you could then identify two or three milestones between now and achieving that future goal.

Once you have formed a clear image and can see the goal with the two or three milestones just ahead of you, I want you to imagine floating up above your timeline so that you're looking down on it. Then, in your mind, move to the first milestone in achieving that goal. When you get there float down into that first milestone and take a moment to experience it fully. What's it like? What do you see and hear and think and feel when you reach that first point of note?

Tip: You can use the submodalities you learned earlier (*see pages 39–40*) to help you fully associate with the milestone so that you can visualize it fully associated (seen through your own eyes): hear what you hear both on the outside and on the inside and then feel what you feel in your body.

Now, float back up above the timeline and move on to the next milestone. Again, I want you to drop down into it, fully associate with it and see, hear and feel everything that you experience there as fully as you possibly can.

Next it's time to float back up above your timeline again and on to the third milestone in the same way and then finally on until the goal is reached. When you have gone to that place where you have already reached the goal, take a moment and in your mind's eye just turn around and float slowly back to the present day, collecting up all the useful learning, feelings and experiences from your future projection and bringing it all back and integrating it into the present day.

Once you are back in the present day, you must remember to turn around (again in your mind's eye) so that you are facing towards your future and ready to take the steps you need to get to where and what you really want.

Here we have worked with going forward from now into the future, but you can use your NLP timeline to rewrite your past just as effectively as you can to pre-write your future. The same timeline technique allows you to change meanings and associations of past bad experiences just as easily as installing empowering beliefs for your future.

Using an NLP timeline

To change your personal history, or at least the way you feel about it, all you need to do is perform the visualization of the past as described in the exercise above. But this time, when visualizing past experiences, imagine yourself floating out of your body and moving towards the direction of your past timeline. This is the past direction that you identified when you elicited your own timelines earlier and as we said is most likely somewhere behind you. But wherever it is, it's yours. As you are moving in that direction, see and feel yourself moving back in time through your own past history and experiences.

Keep on moving in that direction until you feel that you have reached the exact point in time of that particular experience, the one you want to change now. So if you are going back to an experience that happened five years ago, keep moving towards your past direction until you feel that you are at the point of five years ago on your timeline. Give yourself plenty of room so that you don't run out of time/space, and then drain all negative associations from the experience. Visualize washing away all anger, hurt and pain so all that's left is the learning you took from it or, if there wasn't any at the time, what is it now? What are the life lessons to take from it?

Note: When doing this, it is very important to position yourself *above* the experience in your mind's eye so that you are looking down on it. If it's particularly upsetting this dissociation helps reduce the intensity, pain and anger of the experience. And if you remember your submodalities, it gives you a very different *perspective* on the situation and puts you in a position of control over it so that you won't get caught up in the negative feelings instead. From here, you are in pole position to make the changes you need to make and not get bogged down in the associated pain.

When all is done and you can drop down and revisit each of those memories but without any pain, it's time to drift back up above your timeline and all the way back to the present from where you can look back at your past and line up all the past lessons in a row just like a runway. If you are visual, then represent each lesson with a glowing light that will serve you well.

Take it into the future; see/project yourself in the future (by looking towards the future timeline direction). Now push the runway of lessons right out there into the future. See the power, beliefs and abilities developed from the past go into the future you and become integrated with your time to come so that it all feels very new, but very natural. You can take those lessons and use them and live from that place where you have all the resources and resilience from the past right here in the present and future.

As you feel the power of that start to build, you can allow yourself to drift towards the future timeline. See yourself in the future achieving your desired outcomes and becoming the person you really want to be, all fully aligned with the abilities and experience from the past integrated into the future new you. See yourself being stronger than ever and achieving all goals and, of course, see through fully associated eyes so that you can see what you'll see and hear what you'll hear from that place of being fully associated too, so that you can really feel how it feels to live from that place, because this is where you are heading now...

Last, drift back to the present feeling calm and refreshed. Know that your past has given you many great experiences and that your future is looking better than ever. Open your eyes.

This technique effectively integrates both past and future timelines beautifully.

The swish pattern

The swish pattern is one of the best known and most commonly used NLP techniques and you may have come across it before because it is used, and perhaps overused, for a great many purposes by successful people all over the world. You may also have heard it referred to as a 'swoosh' pattern but, however you pronounce it, it's exactly the same thing and is particularly suitable for dealing with one-off situations where you need a confidence boost, or to feel differently about a situation you are about to face, although there are many other times when it may be useful too.

Using the swish pattern

To use a swish successfully, you need to be in a comfortable place where you will not be disturbed. It's better if you are feeling wide awake and alert to do this as it's really quite a dynamic exercise and one that you need to do very quickly for best results. You will have your eyes closed, but you need to be alert and focused during this technique because it's a little repetitive in nature.

Here we are going to take care of a negative or anxious event you have coming up in the near future. I choose the near future because not only will it be a little easier for you to make that picture, but you will also get the chance to experience the positive life-changing effects of the swish pattern sooner and I am all for that, as I'm sure you are too.

Sit comfortably and close your eyes. Take a moment to steady your breathing and relax your body as much as you can and do whatever you know to do to let go of the outside world and any stresses and strains of the day. This is some time just for you; do whatever you need to do, even play some favourite music if you find this helps.

Now, when you are ready, create in your mind's eye an image of you just at the moment of having to deal with the anxiety-causing situation. You'll not have to stay with the bad feeling for long so really go for it and make the image as vivid and sharp as you possibly can. Make it so that it's filling your whole vision, the colours bright, vibrant and alive, with you looking just as uncomfortable as you can possibly imagine. Really go for it and make it seem like an enormous colour slide being displayed on the huge computer screen of your mind's eye. Include anything that will make it more lifelike: other people around you, their expressions, the scenery, sounds, smells, and touch, everything you can think of to make it as real as possible. Like I said, you'll not be there for long, so really go for it.

When you have that picture so vividly that it actually makes you squirm, you've got it about right. We will call that picture the 'time to change'. Giving it a name makes it easy for you to recall later on, but for now, lay it to one side in your mind. In fact, minimize it just like you would on a computer screen; click that little icon and minimize it down to the bottom right-hand corner of the screen.

Now for something much more comfortable. This time, you are going to create an image of yourself just at the moment when you have successfully dealt with the problem, survived it and are feeling really good about it too.

Again, I want you to make it as vivid as is humanly possible and adjust it as before to add in as much detail as you can to make it truly lifelike. Turn the pictures up, make them big and bright and bold and see them through your own eyes. Add in some sound; it doesn't have to be the real sound, just something that makes you feel good. What's your favourite song? Play that and turn the volume all the way up to a level that makes you feel really good. Now take those good feelings and double them in size... then double them in size again and again so that you feel like you are going to burst with good feelings. Make sure that on a scale of one to ten, you are at least above a seven, but the higher the better. We will call this picture the 'preferred reality'. In it, you should be looking absolutely as if you truly have just been incredibly successful with the specific circumstance. When you get it right, when it makes you feel good, allow yourself to enjoy it for a moment, really take it all in... minimize it again just as you did the first one.

Now...

Maximize the 'time to change' picture again, and make sure it fills your entire vision, just as sharp, just as lifelike, just as squirm-inducing as it was before, but with an important addition. The small, black-and-white 'preferred reality' picture is tucked into the bottom right-hand corner. Make sure you can see that before we start.

When you have that image clearly in your mind, just say to yourself, 'S-W-I-S-H' (or swoosh), at the same time changing the pictures over in your mind as quickly as you possibly can so that the 'preferred reality' zooms up to become the large colour picture and the 'time to change' shrinks to the size of a postage stamp tucked into the bottom right-hand corner, becoming black and white as it does so.

Enjoy the good picture and all the good feelings that go with it again for just a few moments.

Next, let your mind drift to some neutral place. This can be anywhere you like – a room in your home, the park, a deserted beach, anywhere as long as it's a place where you are comfortable and at ease. It's very important that you perform this transition to a neutral place each time, so think of somewhere calm and neutral that you can return to, somewhere with no real associations one way or another, a blank canvas if you like.

Now start again at step 1 and continue to repeat the sequence.

1. Maximize the 'time to change' picture again, and make sure it fills your entire vision, just as sharp, just as lifelike, as it was before, but with an important addition. The small, 'preferred reality' picture is

tucked into the bottom right-hand corner. Make sure you can see that before you start.

2. When you have that image clearly in your mind, just say to yourself: 'S-W-I-S-H' (or swoosh), at the same time and change the pictures over in your mind as quickly as you possibly can, so that the 'preferred reality' zooms up to become the large colour picture and the 'time to change' shrinks to the size of a postage stamp tucked into the bottom right-hand corner, becoming black and white as it does so.

After a while, you will find that the pictures change over so easily and so rapidly that you scarcely have any time to see the 'moment of anxiety' before it is replaced with the 'preferred reality'. This can take as few as three or four repetitions and should be repeated over and over until the pictures change instantly right from the start or you find that you simply cannot produce the 'time to change' picture at all.

Remember... real change happens really quickly and so you need use this swish pattern quickly and like you mean it. This is a dynamic change process so it's best to be prepared for it before you start. When you get to the point where change happens automatically, you have successfully programmed yourself for success.

You will find that when you actually get to the event you have been working on, you will feel confident and easy, and able to give of your best as a result. I know it might all sound rather complicated at first, but you soon get used to it and it is worth persevering with; when you take it step by step, you will find that it's actually remarkably simple. It is one of the most powerful 'quick-fix' methods in existence so use it wisely, but as often as you like.

Habits and inner conflict

How many times have you wanted to break a habit yet found yourself doing it on autopilot anyway? How many times have you wanted to make an important decision but found that you just go along with what you have always done anyway, even though part of you knows it's really not right for you?

How many times has part of you known exactly what to do and then another part has gone and done exactly the opposite? This happens a lot in churches: part of you is saying 'I do' while another part is screaming 'but I don't want to'; of course you go along with it anyway because the catering is booked and your mother has a nice new hat. Hardly the stuff that good life choices are made of, but so many people do that all the time and not just with weddings.

Part of you wants to leave your job... but the other part of you is scared; part of you wants to lose weight and be slim, fit and healthy... but another part of you really wants cheesecake, now!

In NLP, you know to listen to language literally, and so for the purposes of the next exercise I want you to literally think of it as a part of you that does, and a different part of you that doesn't, and that this inner conflict between those 'parts' creates that inner conflict in you.

Whether it was a bad habit or an important decision, it's the inner conflict you are experiencing that prevented you from acting the right or, to be completely clear, the authentic way for you. We are all multifaceted and obviously all have free will and choice, but the programming we are running does tend to keep us within certain habitual behaviour parameters. So while one part might well be tugging us in one direction, the other part is keeping us stuck to maintain the status quo.

Now before we get right into it, I want to make something clear. All behaviour at some level has a positive intention and is in fact our brain's solution to another perceived problem. Just think about that... We come into the world hard-wired to be afraid of only two things, falling and sudden loud noises. Everything else is learned either from personal experience or through transference from someone else. But the positive intention is usually to keep us safe.

Think about weight loss for a second... Part of you wants to be slim, but that other part of you still really wants cheesecake. Or what about phobias?

I have treated people for all manner of phobias, from the relatively common, such as spiders and snakes, to the downright weird like bananas, baked beans and, on one occasion, even a phobia of women. Actually, I refused to treat that guy. I told him he'd have more money, be happier and probably live longer if we just left it alone! Obviously, I'm joking... there's no way he'd have more money if he couldn't leave the house lest he bump into a member of the fairer sex. He's fine now, but can you imagine how debilitating that was for him? Of course, part of him knew it was silly, just as part of Dan was curious about what different foods tasted like, but another part of him was terrified to try.

You see how common this is? So common, in fact, that one in ten of the population of almost any country you care to choose has a phobia so severe that it affects their daily lives. Far more therefore have less frequent phobias and even more experience the kind of inner conflict we were talking about earlier. So this is a huge problem... but with a very simple solution. Of course, this is where you are supposed to use a 'strong mind' or 'willpower' to break the habit or take the right action, but as you know, very often, you may not be able to break a habit just because a part of you wants it. If only it were that simple, eh?

Habits and patterns like this are not at all easy to break with willpower alone for one very simple reason. Your brain thinks that it's actually helping and in fact the *problem* is really your brain's *solution* to a different problem altogether.

Think of it like this. The presenting problem is a fear of spiders; you get scared just looking at a picture of a spider. What do you think the positive intention of the fear is? It's to keep you safe from the perceived danger, which makes absolute sense, right? Well, it would if there was any danger there in the first place. Clearly, a picture of a spider is not going to hurt you, but your brain struggles to process that and so instead goes to its primary driver of keeping you safe and acts accordingly. Your brain solves the problem of there being perceived danger by creating a powerful feeling in your body to get you away from the threat and keep you safe. It does make sense when you think about it... only there is absolutely no need for it in the first place because things have got distorted out of all proportion, but we're good at that; we do it all the time.

So by trying to go against the fear with willpower, all we effectively do is create even more inner conflict, which the brain will try to resolve with even more of the same response. You see how that works now?

The more you try to break it, the more this part will hold onto it and so the result will be returning back to the habit, often without you even knowing why. But the more you diet, the more you really want cheesecake, right?

Resolving the inner conflict

Even if you managed to ignore the needs of one of your parts for a while, you will still suffer from the lack of inner integration and will most certainly feel that and a sense of *unease* in your body. You will most likely feel like you are carrying a lot of unfulfilled emotions and unmet desires. I say unmet, but of course, you will be driven to meet them in one way or another, maybe just not quite in the way you would choose – well, not the conscious part of you anyway.

The solution to this inner turmoil is getting more understanding of those conflicting parts then working on uniting or integrating them together with a common goal, which, of course, is your wellbeing. I'm not sure whether this was possible before NLP came into existence, but now integrating those two parts is not just possible, it's actually very easy.

Case study

You might have already seen me use what's called in NLP, 'parts integration' technique on television with the model Katie Price in the UK. Katie had suffered a fear of being out of her depth in water since she had a panic attack in a pool when she was a teenager. Seventeen years on and it took just as many minutes to have Katie in the very same swimming pool swimming completely without fear and enjoying being back in the water again. The footage it available online if you'd like to search for it. Despite being a very 'visual' person in the rest of her life, Katie was 'auditory' and 'kinaesthetic' in her mind and so we used some submodality work and then a parts integration to resolve the inner conflict between the part that wanted to keep her safe and the part that wanted to go swimming.

Parts integration technique

Here's a very simple but quite precise guide for you to follow to integrate those conflicting parts in yourself and others.

The following are the exact steps you should follow in order to unite your conflicting parts under the single common goal of your wellbeing being fulfilled in the best possible way.

Sometimes you will find this technique is also referred to as a 'visual squash' but there are slight differences, so let's get to grips with the original version. Make sure you read all the steps before applying the technique because it's very hard to put things back the way they were once you've done it. Some NLP techniques are reversible; this is not one of them.

Please note that you aren't going to resolve the inner conflict on a conscious level but instead you are going to do it at a much deeper unconscious level. That's why the steps below might require a little bit of imagination.

Step 1: Identify the parts

It's best to do this sitting down somewhere you can safely and comfortably close your eyes and hold both of your hands in front of you so that your palms face the ceiling. Best bet is to familiarize yourself with this then close your eyes and do it; it's quite a trick to read with your eyes closed, even with NLP.

So, palms up with your hands free to move and with your eyes closed, go inside and ask the part that is causing the problem to make itself known to you and to give you a sense of it. Now imagine that part moving out into the palm of your left hand so that you are holding that first part there. Perhaps you'd like to imagine it has a shape and a colour and even a texture.

Some people see it as a glowing ball; some see it as one of their parents and others see much more random things, so just visualize the shape that makes you most comfortable. But if you're not too visual, you may very well get a sense of a feeling in the palm of your hand or a sense that the part has a little weight to it or maybe that it has a sound. Whatever it is like for you, that is absolutely fine and exactly as it should be.

Step 2: Ask the first part about its intention

Ask it for a sense of its positive intention, 'Why do you want to eat that chocolate?' (or whatever it is that you want to change) and notice what comes up for you. The answers will unpack gradually and at first might be something like 'because I want you to enjoy the taste of chocolate'. So then ask it again, 'Why do you want me to enjoy the taste of chocolate?' Perhaps this time the answer will be something like 'because I want you to be happy'. As you ask more questions, you move towards determining the highest positive intention of the part and that is the 'real' reason why you eat chocolate and, of course, the part and the positive intention that we are going to work with and resolve. Keep going until you get to the 'root' of the matter. Don't worry, you'll know on the inside when you've got there.

Step 3: The problem-solving part

Now, we are going to find another part to integrate with the first, or to work with the first in order to fulfil that same positive intention, but only in a way that does not involve sabotaging yourself by eating chocolate.

Now repeat the following as closely as you can remember when you close your eyes: 'I'm talking to the creative, problem-solving part of my own subconscious mind – the part that helps me make decisions every day without my even having to think about it – and asking that part for one new and healthy way to fulfil that same positive intention but without the need for chocolate. I do not need to know what that new way is now going to be, just have a sense of that and when I have a sense of it my subconscious mind can put that part in the palm of my right hand.

You will have a real sense of when that has happened and again, that part may very well be represented by some kind of symbol or image. We are using symbols here because your subconscious mind thinks using symbols, but you may also get some sound or a feeling in the palm of your hand.

Step 4: Bring them/allow them to come together

Talk to both parts and tell them that they both have the same intention for you and that there is no need for any conflict. If you were doing it right from the beginning, you will probably already notice that your hands have already started coming closer together all by themselves. They will continue to do so, guided by your subconscious mind, until they touch; all you have to do is sit there and stay out of the way while your subconscious mind sorts things out for you. Once your hands have touched each other, hold them together firmly and meaningfully and this will send a clear message to your subconscious mind that the conflict is resolved.

If you have performed the technique correctly, of course, you may still eat and enjoy chocolate if you want to, but the subconscious drive to 'self-medicate' with it to change your state will be gone.

In this chapter you have learned three really big techniques. These three patterns, in my experience, can be adapted to work with the vast majority of things that you might want to change in yourself, and maybe others. Just as with anything you'd like to master, the key is in getting them down smoothly so that you don't need to refer back here.

Take some time and go over these techniques again and again. For added effect, start to use what you have already learned about yourself to help you to learn them. If you are predominantly visual, how can you map them out so you learn them in a visual sense? What about if you're auditory? How can you reinforce what I have said so that you get it in sound? And for the kinaesthetic, how can you really get to grips with them and get a feel for what's going on? Go play and have some fun as you learn best.

Chapter 7

Anchoring States

You may have heard the term 'anchoring' used a lot in relation to Neuro-Linguistic Programming. It's right up there with eye-accessing and the swish/swoosh pattern you've just learned in the pop chart of NLP and it richly deserves its place as one of the fundamental and easiest-to-grasp principles. Put simply, it doesn't really matter how skilled you are at making change happen, if you can't make it stick (anchor it), then it's not much good to anyone.

Anchoring refers to the process of associating an internal response with some external (or even internal) stimulus so that the response may be quickly and sometimes covertly, but always automatically, triggered.

In simple terms, think about it like this. You walk past someone in the street and you get a whiff of their fragrance and immediately, and without thinking about it, you find yourself remembering someone close to you who also wore the same scent. It all happened automatically and in a heartbeat. You didn't have to figure out what the smell was and then sift through all the women or men you know until you found a fit and then go and access the memories of those women or men in order to get to that place (well, not consciously anyway); it just happened all by itself. Your subconscious did all that for you so all you experienced was the smell and the associated memory. It's the same thing when a song comes on the radio and it automatically takes you back to a time and place; that song has become anchored to that memory. The song gives you a very fast way to access the memory and so too the 'state' you were in at the time.

Well, if anchoring can do that all by itself, then just as in all other NLP principles, we can model what works naturally and then reverse-engineer it so that we are able to deliberately put this principle to good use for the change that we want in our lives.

NLP Know-how

NLPers did not create anchoring; it is a naturally occurring phenomenon, but with NLP we know how to harness and use it with purpose and for a change. In fact, on the surface, anchoring is very similar to the 'classical conditioning' technique developed by Ivan Pavlov, a Russian physiologist, to create a link between the ringing of a bell and his dogs salivating. (Little is known of Pavlov's cat experiment but I'm sure the results would have been very different!) By ringing a bell while giving his dogs food, he created an association that the bell *meant* mealtime. Pavlov famously found that he could eventually just ring the bell and the dogs would start salivating, even though no food was given.

Think about your schooldays – when the bell rang, you were out of the classroom like a shot – but the main difference between this type of 'conditioning', or stimulus-response conditioning model (as in Pavlov's dogs), and anchoring is that in NLP, the stimulus is always an environmental one (something on the outside) and the response is always a specific behavioural action. The association is considered reflexive and therefore not a matter of choice. But as NLP and our understanding have developed, this type of associative conditioning has been expanded to include other aspects of our experience beyond purely environment ones.

Think back to any sad memory, for example: how do you feel? Sad, right? But here there is no real external factor to make you feel sad, only an internal memory, but it results in a sad feeling in yourself just the same.

Or just as easily, it could be that something becomes anchored to something else that has not really happened. You see an attractive girl or guy in a bar, but instead of the pre-programmed human attraction response kicking in, instead you feel shy, nervous and fearful of rejection, and all you've done is looked up and seen them. You haven't even thought of going to approach them and risk the possible rejection or humiliation yet... or have you?

Or how about in a situation when something went really well, and as you got into the car after closing that big deal, a song came on the car radio, and you now always associate that song with feeling really confident. They have nothing to do with each other really, other than you were in that state and the song was on, but because it was a heightened state, those two unrelated things became joined together in your mind.

Wouldn't that be a great way to feel before you go into the next big meeting? Too right, and so you might want to choose consciously to establish and retrigger these associations yourself so that, rather than being a mindless knee-jerk reflex, an anchor becomes a tool for self-empowerment. How do you think you might do that? We'll get to that in a little while but that song will definitely feature strongly.

A creative tool

As I write this to you, I am sitting at the desk where I sat and wrote all of my previous books. My late mum bought it for me and the lamp that sits on top was also a present from her years before – when the desk was just an aspiration. So as I sit here at my desk in the silence of the early morning with the lamp shining down like it has for hundreds of thousands of words before (all typed with the same two fingers on each hand) with a cup of coffee to my side, do you think it's *coincidence* that I am in the flow and feeling very creative this morning? Of course not... this is where I come to write. To be honest, in between book projects I hardly ever use this desk. It's not for that; it's for this and I hope you are enjoying what it has to offer us both today.

Can you see how this type of anchoring can be a very useful tool for helping to establish and reactivate the mental processes associated with creativity, learning, concentration and lots of other important resources?

NLP Know-how

I have always thought that it is significant that the metaphor of an 'anchor' is used in NLP terminology rather than 'trigger', which I have also heard used. The anchor of a ship is attached to some stable point in order to hold the ship in a certain area and keep it from floating away. The implication of this is that the aspect that serves as a psychological anchor is not so much a mechanical stimulus that *causes* a response, as it is a reference point that helps to stabilize a particular state. The anchor doesn't *cause* the ship to stay in one place; it *enables* it to do so and provides the reference point for that. Whereas with a trigger, you wildly fire off in some direction... I prefer the security of an anchor.

The process of establishing an anchor is very simple and basically involves associating two experiences together so that accessing one enables the other to come about. And in all behavioural conditioning models like this, associations become more strongly established through simple repetition and so repetition can definitely be used to strengthen anchors as well.

For example, my desk didn't just become anchored as my creative place the first time I sat down to write here; it is something that has happened over time. With each hour that's passed and idea that's come, with each good feeling of creating, developing and delivering something that will help and even shape the reader, this space has become very special and creatively significant in my life to the point that while I can write elsewhere, it would just feel so wrong to start a book anywhere else. To be honest, I'm not sure I actually could, well not without some serious internal work to bring the 'state' I'm in now over to somewhere new.

Anchoring and your own learning state

Another good way to begin understanding the uses of anchoring is to consider how they can be applied in the context of teaching and learning. The process of anchoring, for instance, is an effective means of transferring learning experiences. A lot of our learning relates to conditioning, and conditioning relates to the kind of stimuli that become attached to reactions. So if you can anchor something in a learning environment, you can then bring the anchor to the work environment with just a simple reminder of what was learned.

NLP Know-how

In one study, students were taught a new skill in a particular classroom before the researchers split the class in half and put one of the groups in a different classroom – which looked nothing like their original learning environment – then tested both groups. The students that stayed in the original classroom did much better on the tests than the students who had been moved. We can reasonably presume that this was due to subconscious environmental cues, which were associated with the material they had been learning; and in the absence of those factors they found that they had not learned quite so well or were much less able to access the learning they did have. It makes sense, doesn't it?

Now think about this and apply it to children learning in schools right now. If they are anything like me, the 'learning' environment will be anything but conducive to actually learning and I am sure that even now, if you put me back in a classroom like that, I would immediately become dumber and regress back to when I spent more time sitting outside the classroom thinking about what I'd done (or not done) until I was sorry that I actually had learned anything. I wasn't a bad kid, not at all, but I definitely wasn't engaged in school, and those anchors of bad experiences and of 'not learning' when in a classroom stayed with me for many years after I'd left school.

So, with anchoring, we are much more able to stack the deck in our favour. We have probably all been in the situation of experiencing something that we wanted to remember, but when we go into a new environment where all the stimuli are so different, it's easy to forget. We may not have called it anchoring or anything like it, but even simple things like if you take your driving test in the same car you learned in, you are much more likely to pass. And it's not just about knowing where the controls are; it could be exactly the same model but in a different colour and the same is true.

But by developing the ability to use certain kinds of anchors, teachers and learners can facilitate the enhancement of learning. While it doesn't of course guarantee good grades, there will certainly be a greater possibility that learning will be transferred if one can also transfer certain stimuli. Just as I am anchored to writing at my desk even though I have done so now in four different houses, the environment has changed but my being anchored to the desk is fully transferable.

There is another aspect to anchoring, which needs be looked at. It's not good to say that just because you are in a classroom or sitting at a desk you will be able to learn and create just by being there.

In order for the bell to mean anything at all, Pavlov's dogs had to be in a certain state: they had to be hungry so that Pavlov could anchor the stimulus to the response.

If you want someone to learn something, there is no better state to be in than 'curious' because that is when we are naturally most open and receptive. If you are teaching anyone, try this: try opening the interaction with something, anything, that will elicit a state of curiosity. It doesn't really matter what's it's about because it's the state rather than the story that we are interested in.

It's not just for teachers or for doing to others; you can use anchors to re-access resourceful states in yourself. A self-anchor could be an internal image of something that, when thought about, automatically brings on that state. Somebody you are close to, for instance, might immediately bring on the state of love, or fun or compassion. You could also make a self-anchor through an example such as talking about your children or some experience that has a lot of very deep associations.

Establishing an anchor

Pavlov found there were two ways of creating powerful associations. One was through simple repetition, the continual association between a stimulus and a response – the usual way, if you like. The other happens when you connect an intense internal state to a particular stimulus. People, for example, remember the details of highly emotional experiences with no repetition at all. Can you remember your first kiss? Or the death of someone close? People of a certain age can always remember where they were when they heard that John F Kennedy was assassinated or much more recently, on 9/11. Can you remember where you were that day, what were you doing? The association is made immediately, if the state is intense enough, and can last forever.

However, for an anchor to last for a long time, it has to be in some way reinforced, but not to the point where it turns negative. This is absolutely of vital importance. You must anchor when the state is on the way up or at its very peak, but not when it inevitably starts to diminish with time. Pavlov found that if he started ringing the bell and not giving the food, in time, the response to the bell would diminish and eventually stop.

You will also be familiar with that time when you had a new favourite song: you played it over and over again and every time you turned on the radio, it was there too, constantly, to the point where you became sick of it and now, even though it was once your favourite track, you will change the channel as soon as you hear the opening bars. The diagram below demonstrates this:

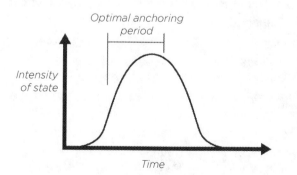

The other aspect has to do with the richness and intensity of the experience one is attempting to anchor.

As an example, imagine that you are preparing for an interview or an important meeting or audition. One of the challenges in this type of situation is in having the ability to articulate what you know, but in an unusual high-pressure environment. For most people the experience is so intense that it's hard to transfer everything you know because the real situation is so different from the one in which you practised and studied. You practised your answers and responses at home in a calm comfortable state, but in the reality of the moment it's a completely different situation that makes it difficult to remember all the things you do actually know.

It's exactly the same for sportspeople: a skilled professional will sink that putt, score that penalty or net that basket 99 times out of 100 in practice. The difference between good and great is being able to do it when the pressure's on and it really matters.

One helpful strategy is to make an anchor. When you are preparing for a pressured situation a great idea is to make an internal anchor, such as a symbol, or something you can touch or hold, like a pen maybe. Practise rehearsing for the big day by running a visualization in your mind's eye of everything going exactly as you would want it to. Make the image as detailed and realistic as you can and make sure you are seeing it through your own eyes, fully associated, and add in any sound and, of course, a calm, relaxed, confident *in-flow* feeling too. All the while you will be holding your pen or simply pressing together a finger and the thumb on your non-dominant hand to create a little 'calm button' that you can use whenever you need it.

I know that lots of sportspeople have a song they play in the dressing room and then in their heads as they go out onto the field and many golfers have a coin in their pocket to rub before an important shot to bring them back into an optimal state. But you must be careful only to anchor good states. I remember watching the TV coverage of the 2012 Ryder Cup: the European team was making its famous final day comeback when on the 16th or 17th green, with the match tied all square, one of the Americans missed a crucial putt to put his European opponent one up with one or two holes to play. He missed the putt and then he critically stayed where he was and took three or four practice strokes with his putter. *It's all over*, I thought. He had just missed one of the most crucial putts of his career and then what did he do with all that adrenaline and disappointment coursing through his body? He anchored missing the putt... and he did it in both senses of repetition of strength and of state. The match was as good as over right there and then. He didn't hole another putt in the match.

You must set up an anchor in 'state', which means the right state. Or become anchored (used to) performing at your best in a heightened physical state and under pressure. How many times have you seen the penalty shoot-out in the World Cup Final and players who could normally score at will miss from the spot when the pressure is on?

Case study

One of the biggest mistakes that people make is to practise in one state and perform in another. This is never more obvious than in the world of sport. I was once asked to help a football (soccer) club prepare for some very big games that would not only define their season, but also have a huge bearing on the financial future of the whole club. For reasons of client confidentiality, I can neither confirm nor deny which club or how big they are but, when I arrived at the training ground, everyone was laughing, joking and 'staying relaxed', as these highly paid precision-kicking machines slotted ball after ball past the hapless reserve goalkeeper in preparation for their big day.

Now fortunately their manager really got it and knew that the difference that would make all the difference was in the mind, not on the field so, one by one, the players lined up at my door: some much keener than others and a few who were only there because they were told to be and would obviously have much rather been anywhere, and I do mean anywhere, *else. Working with the 'state' of each of the players in turn, I collapsed old anchors and associations, effectively wiping the slate clean of bad experiences and negative associations they had built up over their career: that bad miss was vastly reduced or gone, the time they'd missed the crucial tackle consigned to a distant memory. We all have such things; they'll just be very different for everyone. Then I started to install new resourceful, optimum-performance states and anchor them to whatever was specific to that player on match day.*

Now there's one thing I've learned about all sports-people and it's that they do love a routine. Ask any of them which boot or glove they put on first and they'll answer without hesitation. So I set new 'good as new, best version of you in a high-pressure environment' associations and, of course, anchored them to something I knew the players would definitely do. To be effective this had to be specific to each player. For some it was a song, others a smell or pressing together a finger and thumb. Whatever their dominant representation system, we set an anchor there.

Picture the scene in the dressing room at the next game: some pressing fingers, some wearing headphones listening to their favourite tune and some sniffing and smelling their trigger anchor. It didn't matter how silly it all looked, they won and they kept on winning, punching well above their weight and finishing a lot higher in the league than anyone dreamt possible – and beating some of the biggest clubs in the world along the way. Anchoring (if done correctly) can be an incredibly effective NLP tool, but it must be done correctly, and with the best and most resourceful state anchored in the right environment for the right outcome.

As an aside, the England football team have developed a bit of a reputation for being rather terrible at taking penalties. They have gone out of so many competitions when the game has gone to the wire and kicks from the spot. Now you could argue that the way round that would be to just get better so they win the game in regulation time and it never comes to that. But for me the problem is not with their technique, it's in their heads and here's how I would fix it.

When the players practise, they do so in the relaxed environment of the training pitch. The problem is that match day, and particularly the pressure of penalties, is nothing like that at all – and isn't it that pressure that makes the difference? The ones who can handle it will perform very differently from the ones who can't, will they not?

The players need to practise psychologically and get conditioned to performing under pressure. Hell, we know they can all kick a ball; that's why they're signed. But so can the other guys. They don't train for a pressure situation under pressure so that they get used to it. So how do you do that? Well, you find something that matters to them and make it a condition of the desired outcome.

Now, if I know footballers, there are two things that matter to them and they are usually linked: their egos and their cars. I would put both at stake and practise where it matters most to them. If I were to be asked (and you can make up your own mind whether or not I have been) I'd look across the car park to find a rusty heap of a car in the corner, well away from the Bentleys and Porsches (there's always a junior development player, a 17-year-old kid who'll have saved up to buy his only way of getting to training) and this would be the penalty for missing the penalty... Game on.

I'd get the manager to gather the millionaire players around and tell them that whatever I said was gospel for the rest of the session. At that, the little car would lurch round the corner and the groundsman would park it right behind the practice goal. So with the car right in the middle of their visual field, I'd tell them they were all going to take penalties until they missed, at which point they'd have to form another line and earn their way back into the main line – but only when they'd scored three goals in a row (just my way of upping the pressure even further). However, if they were the only one out of the main group when the session ended, they would be driving home in the little rust bucket and the apprentice would be driving home in their pride and joy supercar.

The other thing I know about all sportspeople is that they want to play; they will almost never go against their manager and will do anything they need to do to make the team – no matter what level they are playing at. So, one by one, they'd line up to face the goal and the little rusty car and, one by one, their body language would change and they'd become more serious and, of course, as they did, they'd also tighten up and become worse at football – in the same way they would going into a big game. Now the coaches would have something real to work with.

I don't work with players; I work with states. I know next to nothing about football but that doesn't matter because it's the state that drives the behaviour, just as it does with all behaviour, regardless of where or what that might be.

It's only 'in state' the coaches can really work in a way that would make a meaningful difference. It would not really be so much about the car, although that would certainly put a dent in their street cred, but much more about their ego and not being the one to let the side down, and being teased in the dressing room by all the other guys.

Setting an anchor

An anchor can be set in any of our representational systems and I'm sure, if you think about it, you will be able to find examples for yourself in each. Some of my clients' and mine are visual; for example, I once had a multimillionaire client who felt sick in the pit of his stomach every time he saw an ATM because he associated it, not with his wealth, but with when he was extremely poor and couldn't get any money out. It was this avoidance of pain that drove him every day and still does, I think. For him, it's not the pursuit of wealth that matters but rather the avoidance of being poor.

If your primary representation system is auditory, then a favourite song can immediately take you back to a time and place. If you're more kinaesthetic think of a cuddle that, while very nice in its own way, brings back childhood feelings of being loved, doesn't it? If you're olfactory (smell) dominant then I defy anyone not to feel comforted by the smell of fresh bread baking. I always remember my dad when I smell pipe tobacco. He didn't smoke a pipe, but he took me to football matches when I was a kid and I guess that was the dominant smell on the terraces in those days, so anytime I smell that sweet aroma, I remember my dad. If you're gustatory (taste), then think of a favourite food or taste. In Scotland, for example, we have a dessert called Clootie dumpling – a kind of dumpling with lots of spice and dried fruit that, quite simply, reminds me of my late mum. She would always make one on special occasions like birthdays or Christmas, and after she died, I just couldn't bear to eat it, never mind try to make it. Until this year that is, when Claire and I made Clootie dumpling with my mum's recipe and it was like she was right there in the kitchen with us as I tucked in to my first bite in years... now that's an anchor!

Anchors, as we've said, can be set in any representation system and, put very simply, happen when you bring the 'state' and the 'anchor' together in the same place at the same time.

If I were to make you laugh while touching you on the shoulder at the same time then, given enough repetition in the right state, a simple touch on the shoulder would make you laugh. Simple!

Set an anchor

Try it for yourself. Think of something that makes you feel really, really good and as the good feeling starts to build, just squeeze together any finger and the thumb of your non-dominant hand. Add in your favourite song and turn the volume up in your head to the volume that makes you feel really good. Now take that feeling and double it in size and then double it in size again, all the time keeping your finger and thumb together. Now, release your finger and thumb and repeat those exact same steps a few more times until simply squeezing together your finger and thumb makes you feel really good. Cool, eh?

This was a kinaesthetic anchor (you can feel your finger and thumb together) but you can anchor to any of the representation systems; just choose one that's appropriate for the state you want to anchor.

Conditions for anchoring

Let's summarize the key elements necessary for establishing an effective anchor. They essentially relate to important characteristics of both the stimulus and response you are attempting to pair up and to the context surrounding that stimulus and response.

1. Intensity of response

Intensity is just how fully/strongly a particular state or response has been accessed or recalled. Even during Aristotle's time, around 350BCE, it was known that the more vivid and intense a particular response, the more easily it was remembered, and the more quickly it would become associated with other stimuli. It was easier for Pavlov to 'condition' hungry dogs to salivate than it would have been to condition dogs that had only just eaten, if you see my point.

If a person has accessed only a small amount of the state or experience they are anchoring, the anchor can only be associated with that particular amount of state; it is very much proportional like this. Incidentally and interestingly, 'intensity' does not simply have to do with a person's degree of emotional response. A person may be in a very strong dissociated state, in which they feel little or no emotional reaction at all, and yet can still create very powerful anchors.

Case study
* * * * * * * * * *
I did something very similar for a client, a jockey.
Someone who, despite being an amateur rider and

*having a proper day job, also competes at the very
top level of the sport in group one international races
– nerve-wracking as I'm sure you can imagine. The
horse can very much sense the jockey's state (fear and
nerves usually), so it is vital that these guys, sitting on
top of millions of pounds' worth of racing muscle – and
with even more millions riding on the result (if you'll
pardon the pun) – stay calm before the race. Imagine if
the performance of your car was directly linked to your
state when driving it. Well, it's very much like that in
horse racing.*

*So with Sam, I anchored it so that he got in 'state'
automatically as soon as he put on his goggles before
the start of the race. As soon as he did that and looked
though a different 'perspective', he was 'on' and it
was time to go – he knew it and the horse knew it
too. The anchor fired a change in state in the jockey,
which he then transferred directly to his trusty steed.
Despite being primarily a dentist with a very successful
chain of practices, Sam also won the highly coveted
Cheltenham Gold Cup, one of the oldest and most
prestigious races in the world of horse racing, and in
doing so, established himself as one of the greats of
the sport. Now that's a feeling that's definitely worth
anchoring!*

2. Purity

The 'purity' of the response is largely to do with whether or
not the response, or experience you are anchoring, has been
'contaminated' by other irrelevant or conflicting thoughts,
feelings or reactions. So, for example, if reaching out to

anchor someone with a touch makes them suspicious, or even threatened or uncomfortable, then that discomfort becomes part of the state that is anchored. If you ask a person to think of something positive, but that person is recalling a dissociated memory of the event and, at the same time, judging whether or not they have chosen the right event, you will also be anchoring dissociation, judgement and uncertainty. Simply, whatever their actual internal state at the time becomes anchored – whether they necessarily mean it or not. Does that make sense?

3. The uniqueness of the stimulus used as the anchor

The phenomenon of 'uniqueness of stimulus' relates to the fact that we are always making associations between things in the world around us and our internal states and reactions anyway. Some stimuli are so common and mundane that they make completely ineffective anchors, largely because they have already been associated with so many other contexts and responses and for such a long time. I'm not sure you could really anchor much to the sight of a lamppost or a tree; even just shaking hands is a much less unique stimulus than a touch on the middle digit with the little finger. When was the last time that happened to you? For this reason, unique stimuli make much better and longer-lasting anchors.

4. Timing of the pairing of stimulus and response

The relationship in time between stimulus and response is one of the key conditions of effective anchoring. According to the basic laws of association, when two experiences occur closely enough together a sufficient number of times, the two experiences become associated with one another. Studies involving classical conditioning have shown (rather obviously) that this association only proceeds forward in time: that is, the stimulus (the bell) must precede the response (salivating about food). Fairly obvious, I think.

The concept of anchoring was first introduced in NLP terms by Grinder and Bandler's now classic book *Frogs into Princes* and, although I have used the example of Pavlov to illustrate the point, the primary influence on NLP anchoring appears to have been the great hypnotherapist Milton Erickson, who used his unique voice tonality to create and then deepen trance states in his clients. Through their modelling work Grinder and Bandler discovered Erickson was a master of auditory anchoring and so 'modelled' the pattern in their work on NLP.

In NLP, the optimal anchoring period is determined in relationship to the peak of the intensity of the response or the state you are anchoring. It is generally taught that the act of anchoring should be initiated when the response to be anchored has reached about two-thirds of its peak – see the diagram below for a reminder of the optimal anchoring period.

If possible, the anchoring stimulus should be held until just after the state has stabilized but *before* it begins to diminish. In this way, an association is created between the stimulus and the peak of the response. To do this, the response must be checked, or 'calibrated' as we call it in NLP. Often this can be done by giving the feeling a number between one and ten and checking again when the anchor is being set, then testing it afterwards to gauge how much of the intensity of the state has been triggered by the anchor.

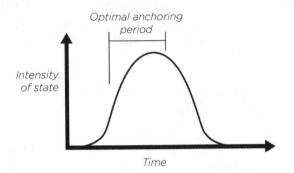

It is best to provide the anchoring stimulus just before the intensity of the response reaches its peak.

5. Context surrounding the anchoring experience
Last, but very important, the context is a critical influence on anchoring and one that is often ignored.

The context, or environment, surrounding an interaction contains many influences, which may affect the anchoring process. Even though they are not the primary focus of attention, environmental cues can also become anchored in what is called 'context association'. Imagine you are anchoring a state of calm and an ambulance with its siren blaring goes past, or you want to anchor the state of being focused but you're in a room with a ticking clock. The general environment may begin to cause a response contrary to that being deliberately anchored.

It is interesting to note that, in this regard, Pavlov first accidently discovered the notion of 'conditioned reflexes' as a result of 'contextual conditioning'. For his research on digestion, Pavlov needed to collect saliva from his laboratory animals. He stimulated saliva flow by placing meat powder in the dog's mouth; soon he noticed the dog would begin salivating simply at the sight of the experimenter, in the expectation of receiving meat powder – a happy accident but not his intention at all.

In some cases, contextual stimuli may combine with the many anchoring stimuli to make the environment part of the overall anchored experience. Because of this, many anchors are 'context dependent'. That is, they work more effectively in the context in which they were initially established.

Exactly as we said earlier, more people pass exams in the classroom where they learned than in a strange room and more people pass their driving test if they sit it in the car that they learned in, because here they are anchored to the context (the classroom or the car), which helps them to access a calm state (they are used to being there) and also is an anchor to accessing the ability itself. It all makes sense when you think about it, doesn't it?

Where do you know you already have anchors set? As with almost everything in NLP, it is reverse-engineered from what happens naturally; here we just have the know-how to 'bottle it' and use these same principles at will. I wonder how quickly you can set a new anchor for something that would be useful to you? If you want to learn more quickly, don't try to cram more in; anchor curiosity and go from there. It's time to think a little bit differently to get what you want. Start with anchoring the right 'state' for the right outcome, and then go from there.

Chapter 8

Meta Model - Deletions

Now before we start this chapter, I would advise you to go and make a cup of tea and delete all memory of English class at school: we are going to be using some of the same terminology but in a very different way. We may well be talking about nouns and verbs and even lost performatives, but before you glaze over, this is going to be an eye-opening rather than eye-closing and *zzz*-inducing section, I promise. So if you're ready, let's delve into the deep sentence structure of the meta model and learn how to turn your life into HD.

Despite what you might have read elsewhere, the meta model is not a series of interrogation-type questions to force people to fill in the missing blanks in the way they describe their problems and the world around them – although it most certainly can be that if you come at it from the wrong place. We know better than that and so we are going to approach the meta model as a language tool for changing our internal map of the world. Remember we touched on this earlier, that we all have deletions, distortions and generalizations in the way we process the world around us (*see page 43*). Well, when working with a client, I am much more interested in uncovering what they don't say than what they do. What they *do* say is only really what's left and what they have got used to including in the story every time they tell it.

What is much more interesting is all the information left out, and the analytical use of the meta model provides us with a number of problem-solving strategies.

We have problems, not because the world isn't detailed enough, but because our internal maps aren't detailed enough.

NLP Know-how

Remember, NLP is a hybrid, a collection of what works, the greatest hits if you like, from lots of other sources, and the meta model is firmly based in the work of Alfred Korzybski, a Polish-American philosopher and scientist. He is best remembered for developing the theory of general semantics. In his work, Korzybski argued that human knowledge of the world is limited by both the human nervous system and by the structure of the language we commonly use.

Korzybski thought that people do not have access to direct knowledge of reality; rather, they have access to perceptions and to a set of beliefs that human society has confused with direct knowledge of reality. Korzybski is remembered as the original author of the phrase, 'The map is not the territory.'

The purpose of the meta model

This model is one of the foundations of NLP as we know it. Our nervous system deletes and distorts whole portions of reality in order to make the world manageable and easier to process and becomes the source code for our behaviour by creating the rules and programs for how we do things – all things.

We delete information to avoid being overwhelmed. But the downside is that we don't see all the choices we have available. We naturally attend to our priorities and overlook other things that we might perceive to be unimportant or not relevant.

We know we also generalize information in order to summarize and pigeonhole what we have experienced. Dealing with categories is much less demanding than dealing with individual bits of information, which all need to be handled separately. Think of your computer; you have folders and within those folders you have subfolders and then files so that you do not need to have every single file on your desktop. So, for example, if we were to have a conversation about cats, we can talk about cats as a category rather than each individual cat that we have ever met or everything we know about cats or every picture of a cat we have ever seen. Instead, we can generalize 'cats' and have a meaningful conversation, even if it does at that level lack a lot of detail.

Last, of course, we distort information as, for instance, when we plan or visualize the future to make goals or even just plan what we are going to do next. Every time we plan anything we are distorting information, we are making up a not-yet-happened reality.

So rather than trying to process all the information we are ever exposed to on our desktop, we create internal maps of the world so that we are able to form a working model of the world around us and know how to behave in that world and in different situations, even those that we have never experienced before. We know how to do that because it's a bit like some other situation we have generalized and stored in a file somewhere. I think you get the idea.

We use these three universal modelling processes to build our maps or models of the world. The terminology used here in NLP comes from the field of linguistics and may seem quite strange, but don't let that worry you. I'm not going to test whether you know all the terms; the important thing is that they make sense, you can spot them in action and know what to do with them. So, let's start with finding what's missing.

Meta model deletions

As we have said previously but is definitely worth recapping, we pay attention to some parts of our experiences but not others. The millions of sights, sounds, smells and feelings in the external environment and our internal world would overwhelm us if we didn't delete most of them, and this is described by Bandler and Grinder as follows:

> 'Deletion is a process by which we selectively pay
> attention to certain dimensions of our experience
> and exclude others. Take, for example, the ability that
> people have to filter out or exclude all other sound in

a room full of people talking in order to listen to one particular person's voice... Deletion reduces the world to proportions, which we feel capable of handling. The reduction may be useful in some contexts and yet be the source of pain in others.[10]

For instance, deleting enables us to talk on the phone in the middle of a crowded station. We tune in to what is important and tune out what we think is not. Just like hearing our name mentioned across the room at a party, it stands out because there is nothing we are more attuned to than our own name, but just as we are also deleting information here, we are doing exactly the same when we think of ourselves as having limited choices. We often overlook problem-solving solutions because we have deleted those options from our internal map.

So let's get straight to it and learn some patterns to help you uncover what's gone missing, give you more choices and recover what was there all along.

Deletion patterns

Unspecified nouns

Unspecified nouns are nouns (a person/being or thing) where you don't know who or what the speaker is specifically talking about. NLP calls this a 'lack of referential index'. Don't you just love these terms? So don't worry about what it's called, unless you want to impress/bore your friends, that is, and just work with it this way.

Not knowing who or what the person is talking about can result in misunderstanding. You (or they) tend to fill in the gaps with your (or their) own ideas. In other words, we don't know so we guess/make up and then act on that guess.

Take, for example, the following phrase, 'They say this is easy.' You could make up 'who' says and 'what' is easy but we don't know. The assumption in this context might be 'people who know about NLP say this meta model stuff is easy', but we don't know that for sure do we? We have just wrapped that meaning around it to make sense in the context of learning about NLP. If we took an equally relevant context, it could be my thoughts on writing this book where 'they' becomes my publisher or even my friends and 'this' is the process of writing.

We often talk about this mythical group of people called 'they', for example:

❖ '*They* won't like me.'

❖ '*They* need to sort it.'

Can you see how this kind of thinking can vastly limit us, when we respond to *them* rather than to real specific people? Some more examples:

❖ The management.

❖ People who don't play fair.

❖ The girls in the office.

Then there's the other part of the deletion (the unspecified verb) in, 'They say this is *easy*' – *What* is easy?

❖ Turning on the computer?

❖ Learning the meta model?

❖ Writing a book?

'I think *they* have lost the plot.' – Who?

❖ The bank?

❖ The government?

❖ Movie producers?

What plot have they lost, a real one or a metaphorical one?

'*It's* delightful' – *What* is delightful?

❖ The weather?

❖ The sarcasm?

❖ The company?

❖ The view?

In short, to recover the deletion you want to find out *specifically* who or what the person is talking about. This word 'specifically' gives us a great little short-cut cheat. Watch...

Questions to recover the missing information

❖ '*Which* members of management specifically?'

❖ '*Management* of *what* specifically?'

❖ '*Which people* do you mean specifically?'

❖   *'Which girls'* specifically?'

❖   *'What* specifically delights you?'

Do you notice a pattern? Good, so that was easy. Now it's time to move from the thing to what it is doing. In English class, we call that the 'verb'.

Unspecified verbs: Understanding the process

Unspecified verbs are the *doing* parts in a sentence that don't fully describe the action taking place. They don't give enough information to let you know what is actually and accurately going on for them. People (which people?) usually fill in the gap with their own experience, a bit like mind-reading.

A simple way to test is this is to ask yourself: are you able to picture the events in someone's statement? If you can't, or the process is fuzzy, there is probably an unspecified verb (or noun) lurking in there somewhere.

Try this: 'He *hurt* me' – so I am trying on different things in my mind like...

❖   He accidentally dropped something on your foot?

❖   He gave you a rude gesture?

❖   He forgot your birthday?

'My boss *frustrates* me.'

❖   Takes too long in the bathroom?

❖   Does not give clear instructions?

❖   Does not promote you when you feel you deserve it?

Their children *behave* rudely.

* Do they make lots of noise?
* Leave the toilet seat up?
* Throw up on your dog?

I'm sure you're beginning to get a feel for this now. OK, so next up, and closely related to unspecified verbs, are what we call 'nominalizations'.

Nominalizations are just unclear verbs that we twist into nouns. Delete then distort. Saying 'I am desperate for *success*' would be an example. Success is not a 'thing'. We can't put it in our pocket or carry it around in a bag yet we make it into a 'thing' to make sense of it – just the same as we do with love, happiness and peace. Of course, to some extent, every verb is unspecified. We would be overwhelmed if we specified everything. What will you gain by having more information on a particular verb? Again, we can use our quick cheat here to quickly recover the missing information by asking,

* 'How *specifically* did your friend hurt you?
* 'How *specifically* does your boss frustrate you?
* 'How *specifically* do they behave rudely?

Simple deletions

Simple deletions are just where part of the meaning is left out or lost. You can notice them in sentences with *the* and *that* and also when referring to missing descriptions (adjectives) – as in 'Please give me *the* report.'

Assuming that you know which category or thing the person means can get you into trouble. You think you know what the boss wants when she says, 'Get me a report on *it* straight away.' You make it up to fill in the deletion gaps. We waste time creating something that quite probably doesn't suit the purpose just because it makes sense in our mind.

Here are a few more:

'I'm so *angry*.'

❖ About world peace?

❖ About my favourite not winning X Factor?

❖ About being tricked out of everything I own?

'I broke my *promise*.'

❖ To be home on time?

❖ To love, honour and obey, forsaking all others till death do us part?

❖ To climb Mount Everest before I was 40?

Notice how *specifically* one little word can get us right back to all the information we need so very quickly.

❖ Questions to recover the missing information would be:

❖ '*What specifically* are you angry about?'

❖ '*Which* promise *specifically*? To *whom specifically*?'

Comparative deletions

Comparative deletions are actually hypnotic words with which we make a comparison but don't explain what we are comparing. There is some kind of standard or judgement involved, but it isn't made *specifically* clear.

When you accept a judgement without understanding what's behind it, you can get stuck. Many self-esteem issues come from deciding someone is better or more worthy at a general level rather than questioning the standard. 'Better at *what* specifically?' If you don't know what the standard is, how can you ever measure up to it?

Vague unquantified comparisons use words like better, best, harder, faster, stronger, improved, more, less, very, bigger, smaller, brighter, louder, healthier, superior, smarter, enhanced. You'll find that marketers love these terms. They slip in a percentage together with the comparison so it sounds more credible. (Did you spot the deliberate deletion – more credible than what?)

'Get 20 per cent better hair with new improved Hairie-poo.'

* Better than old unimproved Hairie-poo?
* Better than what? Washing in muddy water?
* Better than the market-leading alternative?

'Burgers are bigger and better at Sam 'n' Ella's café.'

* Bigger than what? The cockroaches in the kitchen?
* Bigger than at the place next door?
* 1 per cent bigger or 95 per cent bigger?

'Buy our double-strength adhesive!'

- ❖ Double the strength of what? Jam?
- ❖ Double the strength of welding?
- ❖ Now it lasts two days instead of just one?

'He is much more intelligent.'

- ❖ More intelligent than what/who?
- ❖ Than the average conifer?
- ❖ Than the average Mensa member?
- ❖ Than all the other applicants for the job?

Questions to recover comparative deletions:

- ❖ Better than what *specifically*?
- ❖ Bigger than what *specifically*?
- ❖ Double the strength of what *specifically*?
- ❖ More intelligent than who or what *specifically*?

Without wishing to sound like Donald Rumsfeld and his 'unknown knowns' and 'known unknowns', it really does help to be aware of what isn't there. Or at least isn't said. We use language very literally, but really paying attention not just to what is said but also what is assumed and what is deleted, I hope you can see that we can very quickly start to uncover how someone is creating their map and experience of the world. Understanding the meta model and challenging (gently) some of these distinctions not only helps to enrich our understanding, but also the other person's too. It's a little like turning the picture into HD so that you can see what's always been there but just wasn't obvious. The more you are aware, the more choice you have, simple as that.

Please don't worry whatsoever about the terminology in this section. That's not the important part. What is important is that you get, and begin to see and hear, what's missing, every bit as much as what is there. Very often the key is in the unspoken word, in what's being assumed when that assumption can be very limiting indeed. Assume nothing... Go find out.

Chapter 9

Meta Model – Generalization Patterns

Next up in our whistle-stop tour of NLP, and still very much within the meta model, is what we know as 'generalization patterns' or 'universal quantifiers'. Again, you will spot what's going on here from everyday conversations. I will give plenty of examples so you don't even need to think about the terminology; just allow yourself to notice how many you already know once they are pointed out to you. But this is how Bandler and Grinder describe generalization patterns and the reason why we should be aware of them:

> 'Generalization is the process by which elements or pieces
> of a person's model become detached from their original
> experience and come to represent the entire category
> of which the experience is an example. Our ability to
> generalize is essential to coping with the world... The same
> process of generalization may lead a human being to
> establish a rule such as, "Don't express any feelings."'[10]

When using universal quantifiers, you are effectively saying, 'There are no exceptions and therefore there are no choices either.' And of course, we already know that this is almost never the case, but sometimes it can be useful to frame things like this as in, for example, 'You will *always* find a way if you persevere.' But most of the time, we will be challenging these universal quantifiers, to unpick the scope for change that you didn't even know was there.

The biggest problem with this kind of language pattern is that it creates limitations for us. We don't even look for a solution because we assume there isn't one. We can severely limit ourselves, especially when it comes to the scope of the language we use in our minds.

Hypnotizing into belief

Language matters. Think about it this way: at a very simple level, let's suppose we didn't have a word for something. How do we know how to treat it? Then let's say that we have a very limited scope for expression – let's say we only have the words happy and sad – does that mean that we can only operate in those parameters?

Case study

Writing this reminds me of a time I was invited to dinner in Abu Dhabi with some eminent literary people, not my natural habitat at all, and as I sat listening (in the most intelligent manner I could muster between yawns... it was the jetlag, honest!) to conversations about books I'd not even heard of, let alone my preference for which language they translated into

*best, my little brain went whirling off to try to find
some common ground on which I could actually
contribute to the conversation.*

*What happened next, though, was quite remarkable.
I didn't consciously realize I was using my NLP
knowledge, but when you join the dots you'll see what
happened. I pieced together the different parts of the
conversation and got to thinking, 'If the same book
is translated into a different language, how is it that
someone can have a preference for one over the other?
Surely you would just prefer the one written in your
native tongue?'*

*When I put that to the group, they all (and at great
length) explained that this was not the case as
some languages are far more full and descriptive
than others, so when a book is translated from an
expressive language like English or French to a less
flexible language like Arabic, many of the subtleties
and distinctions will be missed as the language just
doesn't have the scope and breadth of expression.
The opposite is also true and translations between
languages may also add more description and enrich
the text with a greater depth of emotion and feeling.
I had taken for granted how deep and descriptive the
English language really is; just like the Inuit people have
many different words for snow, in Scotland, we have
just as many for rain.*

So, if it's the case that the flexibility and scope of the
language affects the experience of reading the book, is
it also true of the people who speak the language and

their experience of the world around them? So if you have limited scope for distinction and lots of generalizations, is it not therefore just as likely that you will be missing out on lots of choices? You see my point?

Universal quantifiers to look out for are words such as 'all', 'every', 'never', 'always'.

When you hear these words, the person (or yourself) is clearly showing you their beliefs. Pay attention when you use them, particularly if it's to do with a problem you've had for a while. How often do you hear yourself say things like...

❖ 'I'll *never* get this right.'

❖ 'The *world* is against me.'

❖ 'I *always* try to do my best, but she just hates me.'

❖ 'He *never* listens to me.'

I'm sure some of these are all too familiar to you, just as they are to most people the world over, regardless of their native language. This is simply because we do all like to generalize and simplify how we process the world to make sense of it. But just as before, it is not in what's said that we find the useful distinctions; it's in what's not. **It is always far more powerful to see something new than to see something old yet again.**

Try some of these 'recovery' or 'uncovering' questions and see how much more detail and choice you can add with just a few well-chosen words.

❖ 'Has there ever been a time when I did get it right?'

❖ 'You mean every single person in the whole world is against you? Everyone?'

❖ 'How do you know she hates you?'

❖ 'So he (who is he?) has never listened to you about anything, ever?'

I'm sure you get the idea of how this works. Now we're going to move on to one of my personal favourite patterns and show you just how quickly you can change the way you feel about something by using even just one single word. Before we do this, though, I want you to pay particular attention to your feelings.

❖ How do you feel inside right now?

❖ What one word would you use to describe your own internal experience?

❖ How quickly do you think you could change that feeling?

Let's play with some modal operators and find out.

Modal operators – another meta model generalization

The term 'modal operators' might sound a bit odd but it simply refers to 'your mode of operating'. Modal operators are just words like 'must', 'should', 'can't', 'have to', 'mustn't', 'can', 'will' and, in fact, 'just' itself, and all indicate possibility or necessity. There is a big difference between doing something because you feel you *have* to or you *should* or because you *want* to. Just changing that one word makes a world of difference in how you feel about it, doesn't it?

How often do we feel as if we *have* to do certain things and have no choice? At those times, we tend to use words such as 'should', 'must', 'have to', 'need to', 'ought to'. Operators of implied necessity most often create stress states that are self-imposed and almost always disenabling in some way. But a further problem presents itself with the use of implied necessity modal operators. We very seldom really question whether we actually *have* to do certain activities or feel a certain way; we just sort of assume that we *should* and so we act from a place of limited or no choice when the reality can be very different.

Most of the time, we don't stop and examine the real consequences of not doing those things. Instead, we just carry on with the sense of being hard done by. This is probably most obvious when you hear other people use these words in a context you wouldn't.

❖ 'I *have* to tidy the house before Claire gets home.'

❖ 'I *should* be home in time to go to the gym.'

❖ 'I *must* get this chapter finished today.'

As with all meta model patterns we are going to work with, there are some very simple recovery questions that enrich the experience and add so much more choice than if we just accept the statement at face value as an absolute.

Notice when you spot others using and misusing modal operators and try a few simple questions to see what happens next. The best way, as with all this stuff, is to play with it in the real world. NLP is a practical subject reverse-engineered from what happens naturally anyway, so have a play and see how you get on and what you discover when you ask...

❖ 'What would happen if you didn't?'

❖ 'What would happen if you did?'

❖ 'What would be the consequences?'

States of necessity drive us to meet deadlines for sure. I might very well stay up all night to finish this chapter and meet my self-imposed deadline, but there is no real *need* to do so. Nothing will happen if I do, and nothing will happen if I don't. The only possible use I could have for this modal operator is to impose a motivator of fear on the proceedings and I'm not sure how that's going to help anyone.

But, of course, that is exactly what many people do to help them focus all their resources to reach important goals. Many find it motivating, but it will only really ever be in an away from 'pain' sense, in the sense that there is an implied threat of something bad happening if you don't and so to avoid that pain, you force yourself to do the task, not for the benefit it will bring you, but for the avoidance of pain if you don't. Effective it may be, but stressful, it definitely is. There is a big difference between, 'I'd like to make extra money this month' and 'I *have* to make extra money this month'. Or what? Says who?

Necessity-type thinking diverts us away from other much more important and useful outcomes by creating a kind of tunnel vision. You will often hear people talking about being focused on their goals, but if you take a slightly different perspective on this, you will see that being focused on your goals as you see them and, more particularly, your perceived route to achieving them, automatically and by its very definition rules out all the other options.

Now, add into the mix that you know our perceived choices are always passed through the filter of our personal experience and then subject to deletions, distortions and generalizations, and you will see that just thinking *it is* the right or best way to do something gives you very little guarantee that it actually is. Surely it would be much better to stay open to the best way and to new opportunities as they present themselves rather than be blinkered on the other way at all costs.

In my experience in looking after some of the world's most successful people, **a goal can never be as powerful as an inspiring idea.**

One is outside in and the other is inside out. It's a bit like *want to* versus *should*. Just try those yourself right now. Which is more powerful and motivating, a *want to* or a *should*? Well, in my experience, people never need a pep talk or a motivational seminar to do something that they actually *want* to do in the first place. But with *should*, they try to find tools and ways (NLP included) to get themselves to do things that they think they *should* do but don't really *want* to.

If you want your life to change quickly, don't set any more goals. Instead, focus on doing things that make you feel inspired and when you are inspired, go and do that instead. That's after all what you *want* to do. I have never met anyone who needs motivating to collect their lottery winnings – coincidence? I think not.

'People are always gonna try to tell you how to run your life; great, listen to them but follow your heart and you'll last forever...' I think this quote was the first piece of self-help advice I ever read and one that has served me well. It did not come from some guru in a book either; it was in the notes for Lita Ford's album *Lita*, which was one of my favourite albums at the time.

I did not meta model it back then, but if I had it would have gone something like this. 'People [*which people?*] are always [*really always?*] gonna try to tell you [*who?*] how to run your life [*all of my life, in every aspect?*]; great [*is that really great, says who?*], listen to them [*everything 'they' say, always?*] but follow your heart [*where? How do I do that?*] and you'll last forever...'

We can pick anything apart with the meta model but please don't, words can be wise even if they are not semantically complete and how we interpret them can be very good as well as very limiting; that choice is always (yes, always) yours.

OK, more meta...

Modal operators of impossibility

We often talk about things as though they are impossible to achieve or do. Our unconscious accepts these as therefore automatically real limitations. These are words such as 'can't', or 'impossible'.

❖ 'I just *can't* find love.'

❖ 'I just *can't* get up in the morning.'

❖ 'It's *impossible* to talk to her.'

And as you might expect by now, there are some really rather obvious ways to cheat your way to uncovering more useful information and enriching the person and your own map of the world. The information is there; it has just been generalized and with these questions we are, in effect, just zooming in to gain more detail. Try out these simple recovery questions to get your zoom fired up for all the detail and distinctions you'll ever need.

❖ 'What stops you?'

❖ 'What would happen if you did?'

❖ 'What would happen if you could?'

And then my personal favourite,

❖ 'What's that all about?'

Simple, I know, but you will be amazed at what comes up.

With me so far? Good. Well, the next is perhaps the trickiest of patterns to get your head around in the abstract so again I will make it as easy as possible with a few real-life examples.

Complex equivalences

Again, don't worry about the fancy title. Complex equivalences involve constructing beliefs out of generalizations and linking two experiences together for no real reason other than we think that way. However, it can feel very, very real and restrictive until you shine the spotlight of a few recovery words on it.

Case study

For example, someone may believe that another person's not making eye contact means they have something to hide or that they don't like them. I did a huge NLP event recently and in the audience was a guy who had actively gone out of his way to avoid a co-worker for four years because, on his first day at the job, this other person had not made eye contact with him as they passed in the corridor. My guy instantly formed the assumption and then belief that there was a problem between them. Nothing had actually happened to prove it other than he had enough evidence for himself so he never questioned it... right up until the guy in question got in the lift with him and said, 'We've never really spoken; I wondered if you didn't like me for some reason. I hope that's not the case because I can't think why.' Sometimes it is a pretty weak link, but it makes sense to the person at the time even if it doesn't to anyone else, not even the person involved.

Uncovering the things we've made equal can be incredibly liberating.

❖ 'I got the big deal; my problems are definitely over.'

❖ 'If you haven't made it by the time you are 30, you never will.'

- ❖ 'He didn't smile at me; he doesn't like me.'

- ❖ 'I didn't get the job; they don't respect women.'

So, that's the pattern; let's get straight to the quick recovery questions.

- ❖ 'How does the big deal solve your problems?'

- ❖ 'How specifically is age related to wealth?'

- ❖ 'How is smiling related to liking?'

- ❖ 'If they respected women, would they definitely have given you the job?'

Again, the best place to practise these is in the real world. Go and play!

I wonder how much and how quickly your life could change if you didn't just jump to those kinds of conclusions. Just because you think it and even if it 'makes sense' does not mean it's true... This is something to think about, and yet another way to experience a small change making a big difference.

Chapter 10

Meta Model – Distortions

The third key element to the meta model are 'distortions', which are responsible for some of the most major limitations and the creation of some very limited internal maps of the world. Anything we make up, or that we have no sensory evidence for is a distortion.

Maybe you're thinking, 'I don't make things up, I am a very down-to-earth person'. But think about this... often we have to make something up – in fact, in order to understand and make sense of anything that has not yet happened, we have to make up how we think it will be. Everything from a holiday to wanting to get married or have a family or planning for retirement has to be constructed in order to make sense of them. And to construct them, you have to make them up of the bits and pieces you have lying around in your personal experience of how you have experienced things so far and how you have experienced them through other people. In other words, you simply have to create a map of how you think the world will be one day and then plan for that.

NLP Know-how

Richard Bandler and John Grinder defined meta model distortions thus: 'Distortion is the process which allows us to make shifts in our experience of sensory data. Fantasy, for example, allows us to prepare for experiences which we may have, before they occur... It is the process which has made possible all the artistic creations which we as humans have produced... Similarly, all the great novels, all the revolutionary discoveries of the sciences involve the ability to distort and misrepresent present reality.'[10]

Distortions are responsible for some of the most major limitations and the creation of some very poor maps. Anything we make up, or that we have no real sensory evidence for, is a distortion. For example, have you ever *speculated* about what might be causing the traffic jam or the fault with the TV or why that person hasn't emailed back or called? I bet you have and unless you know for sure, you are making it up; we call that a 'distortion'.

The two best illustrative examples of distortions are future planning and our creation of concepts.

Consider what happens when you make choices about your future, or even just plan a holiday. You are thinking about a future that does not exist, yet. You literally cannot see yourself retired or on holiday unless you already are. We cannot possibly see a picture of something that hasn't happened yet, unless we make it up.

But, of course we can do that very easily when we can visualize future consequences, experiences and benefits in our imagination.

But remember, just because you think it does not make it true; we just sometimes think it does.

The creation of concepts

A concept is something we humans make up. Have you ever left the house and just tripped over a relationship? A relationship is a concept and consists of a number of on going interactions and shared experiences over time (another concept). Can you put a relationship in a wheelbarrow? Of course not!

We use labels for concepts, but there is no sensory-based evidence for them. There are certainly examples of them, but we make up the label for the concept. It's like a shorthand marker to guide us, but it really only works if we are all working to the same version of the concept. Otherwise, even with the same terms, we can end up in a very different place. How many different types of relationships can you think of? Do they all adhere to the same rules and conventions? No...

Take the idea of your favourite party. Is that a birthday party, political party or a third party? It's whatever you mean it to be, but it might not mean that same thing to me. Here are some of the key meta model patterns for distortions.

Nominalizations – recipes for misunderstanding

Linguistically speaking, nominalizations are processes (verbs) we turn into nouns. But doing this sends deceptive messages to our brains. For example, a 'decision' is actually the process of deciding; a relationship is the process of relating to someone. In both, there has to be some 'doing' in order for them to exist, but by changing the process into a fixed static 'thing', we can feel it as a tangible entity when, in effect, it is something you have to do. You might remember we spoke earlier about depression (see pages 75–76) being a thing someone does, rather than a 'thing' that you might catch. This is exactly what I am talking about here.

Nominalizations give the sense that something is real when, in fact, it is not and creates lots of scope for misunderstanding. Some popular concepts are:

- ❖ Relationship
- ❖ Decision
- ❖ Success
- ❖ Motivation
- ❖ Stress

What do you think the recovery questions might be? Well, how about these?

- ❖ 'The problem is my relationship.' – How are you relating?

- ❖ 'The decision is final.' – What are you deciding? How have you gone about deciding? What's that process like for you? If I had to decide the same way you do what would I need to do?

- ❖ 'I want to be successful.' – How will you know when you are? How do you know you're not already?

- ❖ 'My motivation isn't what it used to be.' – What do you want to motivate yourself to do? How do you do motivation?

❖ 'I have a lot of stress in my job.' – What is pressuring you? How are you stressing? How do you do stress?

This pattern is one of the most important problem-solving strategies in the whole meta model. Nominalizing and therefore making things into a static unchanging thing causes many difficulties, but as you might be beginning to see, they are not real... well, not unless we act on them and make them real, of course. But while they only exist in the world of the mind, you are only ever one thought away from being well again.

The next pattern is one of my absolute pet hates. Have you ever spent time with someone who is certain that they know best when you actually do know best? This is similar to the above, but here we really just making s**t up, jumping to conclusions or mind-reading. We'll stick to this title for the sake of the book but know that I really mean making s**t up.

Mind-reading or jumping to conclusions

Mind-reading is assuming you know what the other person is thinking or feeling without checking for any real evidence. This pattern causes a great number of interpersonal problems, the awareness of which is another of the important meta model problem-solving strategies.

Most of us, at some time, attribute intention to other people's behaviour or absence of behaviour. We think we know that someone is interested in us, doesn't like us or is trying to hurt us, without their ever saying so.

We are masterful at taking a small cue such as a raised eyebrow, a lack of eye contact or a failure to do something we expected and believing we know what it means. We all jump to conclusions about other people's behaviours at some time. We usually judge others' behaviour by the effect on us, and judge our own behaviour by our intentions.

We also expect other people to be able to read our minds. We think someone should know we are pleased or annoyed with him or her. We expect others to realize we are overwhelmed, open to suggestion or distracted.

The meta model questions aim to uncover how you know what you think you know about what is happening in someone else's brain.

Some examples are:

* 'I know you don't want to come to my party.' – How do you know?

* 'I know you think I'm…' – How do you know that?

* 'The boss doesn't think I am promotion material.' – How do you know that?

Cause and effect – not really how our world works

When someone uses a cause-and-effect statement, they are identifying how they believe something works, that X causes Y, or that doing X makes Y happen.

The next pattern is one that you will notice all the time as soon as I point it out and is probably one of the areas that , even after just reading through it once, you can easily start to use to make changes in the people around you.

How often have you heard someone say some version of this/that/they made me do it?

* 'I had a stressful day so I had a doughnut on the way home.'

* 'My meeting went badly so I stopped at the pub on the way back to the office.'

* 'They hurt me so I ...'

These are all cause-and-effect dynamics and, of course, completely constructed, even though they make perfect sense to the people at the time.

Cause and effects are statements that show how someone believes something works. Like all beliefs, just because we believe something, it doesn't make it true. Often looking at our statements can open us up to solutions we hadn't considered because we start questioning our model of the world.

Let's look at a few more 'if–then' statements:

* 'If I give my children everything they want, they will love me.'

You'll notice that they usually have words such as 'forces', 'makes', 'creates', 'leads to', 'compels', 'requires', 'instils' and 'causes'. For instance,

* 'Going into business requires a lot of capital.'

* 'Violent video games lead to a high crime rate.'

A cause-and-effect-type distortion that is often made is assuming that someone can make us feel a certain way.

For example,

- ❖ 'You made me so angry.'
- ❖ 'You exhaust me with your constant whining.'
- ❖ 'I won't be happy until you are home.'

This assumption acts in reverse too. Feeling responsible for the state or happiness of others is a common and debilitating belief. For example,

- ❖ 'I know I can make him happy.'

You can't, only he can make himself happy; you can help but you cannot *make* him happy.

This next pattern is the one that took me the longest to get my head around, so let me try to make it as simple as I had to for myself. If I got it, then you will straight away.

Lost performatives – not my beliefs

Lost performatives are when someone is talking about a personal belief, but presents it as though it were a universal truth. We then accept it as true without questioning it, as we would if we heard it as someone's personal opinion. Lost performatives equals not my 'beliefs' – it's a fact!

These might be clichés that *everyone* knows are true. Even though some of these truisms are useful, the origin is lost, so they are disconnected. For example,

- ❖ Vitamins are an essential part of a healthy diet.
- ❖ Knowledge leads to power.

❖   If it's meant to be, it will happen.

The danger of these lost performatives is that they bypass our reasoning filters. We can take on these ideas as beliefs and delete perfectly good solutions to our problems. We don't think *which* circumstances they apply to or consider whether they apply to *all* people

The origin is important too. Politicians, marketers and salespeople all use these techniques. But how many of these studies are promoted by people with a vested interest? Of course, the company is going to say their product is good for you. What else are they going to say? 'Humans can't actually digest our stuff; we only used to feed it to pigs, but if we tell you it's healthy then the sales skyrocket.' It would be refreshing, but unlikely.

Here are your lost performative recovery questions.

❖   Who says?

❖   For whom is this true?

❖   According to whom?

We want to find out where the belief came from and whether the strategy is based on something solid.

Linguistic presuppositions

Presuppositions are the most powerful of the meta models and the Milton Erikson model language patterns are some of my favourites – perhaps because they are heavily and widely used in hypnotic patterns, but mostly due to the fact that they are one of the most simple and elegant ways to guide someone in the direction that you want to take them. And as a communicator wouldn't it be great if people sometimes accepted what you said without question?

For example, a couple of favourites with parents are,

- ❖ 'Do you want to go to bed now or in 30 minutes?'
- ❖ 'Do you want to tidy your room before or after dinner?'

There is an illusion of choice, but both choices get your outcome. Of course, as we get older and smarter, we see through some of the illusions (or do we?)

Unfortunately, this power can be used for bad as well as good. We probably have no idea of the kinds of things we take for granted in order to make sense of someone's communication or to create a well-formed sentence.

They can also take away our sense of choice when we use them on ourselves, or when others use them. We can feel painted into a corner.

- ❖ 'Have you stopped being so noisy?'
- ❖ 'Have you learned to control your temper yet?'
- ❖ 'When did you get so bossy?'

Linguistic presuppositions of existence

This next one is the simplest kind of presupposition, for example:

- ❖ 'Bob ate the pancakes.'

This presupposes that someone named 'Bob' and that indeed a number of pancakes exist. We accept these things and our focus is on the action of eating. Bob and the pancakes are in the background but very much there and very much taken as read.

Linguistic presuppositions of awareness

Here we are not questioning the second part of the sentence. This is a useful pattern:

❖ 'Do you realize you are the first person to get 100 per cent?' – There is no question of the grade, just whether you realize.

❖ 'You may notice a small button on the left.' – There is a button; you just have to find it.

❖ Are you aware you are already in trance?' – You are in trance; you just need to be aware of it.

Linguistic presuppositions of time

These include the use of time or change of time words like 'begin', 'end', 'before', 'after', 'during', 'future', 'when', 'again', 'still' and 'soon'. While particular tenses – such as 'was', 'had', 'been', 'went' (past); 'am', 'have', 'are', 'stop', 'start', 'continue' (present); and 'will', 'going' and 'getting' (future) – can all create very powerful assumptions.

❖ 'Would you mind taking the rubbish out before you tidy your room?' – You are tidying your room.

❖ 'Are you still drinking?' – You have been drinking; the only question is whether you have stopped.

❖ 'I saw her at the window again.' – She has been at the window previously.

Linguistic presuppositions of order

When we use words such 'first', 'once', 'second', 'twice', 'last', 'another', 'again' and 'next', we are presupposing a series of things.

❖ 'My second wife is really funny.' – This presupposes a first wife and perhaps one who wasn't very funny.

❖ 'My first husband liked football.' – This presupposes husband number one is no longer a husband for whatever reason, that there may be subsequent husband/s, *or* that she intends to get married again sometime.

When we really listen to language carefully words can be insightful like this – often the person is using them unconsciously. (For example, in the second example, she may not consciously have considered remarrying.)

This OR the other, but definitely one of them

Here we exclude one thing or the other.

❖ 'Would you like white or wholemeal bread?' – You are getting a sandwich.

❖ 'Would you prefer to pay by cash or cheque?' – You are paying for something.

'Do you want to pay for this now or when we deliver it?' – There is no question of payment, only when.

'Do you want to go to the gym at the end of this chapter or once you've done the whole book?' – I am going to the gym; it's just a matter of when.

Adverbs and adjectives

The 'ly' adverbs

These are really just words with the suffix 'ly' on the end, such as 'unfortunately'. I have to admit I didn't pay much attention to those 'parts of a sentence' things in English class. In fact, I didn't pay much attention too much at all in school, but this is the simplest explanation I can give you.

The 'ly' adverbs are sneaky things, because they modify or change the standard verb and so are just assumed and accepted to be true, and they slip under our radar. We tend to accept the sentence without questioning whether it is true. For example:

❖ 'He quick*ly* moved the files to the other drawer.' – What was quick about it? The focus is on the quick rather than the nature of the files or where they now were. We focus on the quickly and maybe wonder why, but the rest is accepted as a given.

❖ 'I clear*ly* did not want it to rain today.' – Why was it clear? What was clear about today?

❖ 'Obvious*ly*, we don't want to pay the amount you are asking.' – What is obvious about it? Once again, it presumes that it is unquestioned that the price is too high and everyone would feel the same.

❖ 'Regrettab*ly*, I want you to finish by 5 p.m.' – What is regrettable about it? It says, 'I don't really want to ask this of you, but I am going to anyway and it isn't my fault.' It makes a demand seem less demanding. And what is finished by 5 p.m., the task or your career?

❖ 'Fortunate*ly*, I remembered and went back for it.' – What is fortunate about it? It lets the fact that you messed up and forgot it in the first place slide past almost unnoticed.

These 'ly' adverbs and other descriptive words presupposing certain qualities, such as 'just', 'only', 'even', can be particularly misleading and dangerous.

❖ 'It's *just* about perseverance.' – Is perseverance really a simple thing?

❖ 'He is *just* the driver.' – Dismisses and discounts this role.

❖ 'My friend is *just* as cheerful as her mother.' – Apart from the existence of the friend and her mother, we don't question the mother's cheerfulness.

❖ 'You *only* have to babysit for an hour.' – Dismisses the chore as short-lived.

❖ 'He was annoyed with me, *even* though I worked really hard.' – The other person is being unreasonable.

Using the meta model effectively

How *specifically* do you do that?

The meta model very simply but brilliantly provides a framework to recover deleted but very useful unspoken information and, in doing so, uncovers our subconscious *rules* while untangling misunderstandings in our own and others' communication.

Specifically, it helps to fill in the missing pieces of our map to add more detail and distinctions, a bit like turning up the resolution on the map and, in doing so, turning our map into HD. Imagine your TV picture and then imagine it in HD. The subject is still the same; if you're looking at a garden then you're still looking at a garden in HD, only now you can see much more detail and therefore, when it comes to making changes, you have much more choice.

The more distinctions you are aware of then the richer your map of the world; and the richer your map of the world the more choices you have in your life, and so the richer your life will be... Simple.

Meta model questions

By listening for how someone has created his or her map, we can ask an appropriate question to recover what has been deleted, generalized or distorted. This then expands and enriches the person's choices for solving the problem. You with me?

As a simple guide, you will find that the *cleaner* you are in yourself, the easier you will find working with the meta model. In other words, the fewer assumptions you make yourself and the fewer preconceptions you bring to the interaction, the easier it will be to spot the part of the map that is missing. I cannot emphasize this enough; the *cleanness* of your own ability not to make things up makes it much, much easier to spot it in others. But if you are filling in the blanks yourself, then it is very difficult to know that there is a blank there in the first place.

First rule of meta modelling – assume nothing, and then *specifically* ask the right question to uncover 'their' missing part.

Here's a quick guide to help you get going and to get to grips with using the meta model effectively.

Deletions: The missing parts of the model

As we learned earlier, information is deleted in six main ways.

1. Unspecified nouns

Any word that stands in for a noun and so has many meanings and interpretations.

✦ 'They say this is easy.'

Don't assume. ASK: '*Who* says that *what* specifically is easy?'

2. Unspecified verbs

Verbs that delete the specifics of the process.

✦ 'My friend hurt me.'

Don't assume you know. ASK: '*How*, specifically?'

3. Nominalizations

Verbs that are made into nouns, and thus delete the process or action and so very often create a sense of *stuckness*, but can often be recovered just by adding 'ing' and turning it back to a verb.

❖   'Our *relationship* just doesn't work any more.'

ASK: 'What specifically about the way you're relat*ing* causes you to think that?' Turn the nominalization back into a verb again.

4. Lack of referential index

The pronoun is not specified, and so deletes who or what it refers to.

❖   'People love chocolate.'

ASK: 'Who *specifically* loves chocolate?' And even, 'Says *who*?'

5. Simple deletions

Information is simply missed out.

❖   'I'm so upset.'

ASK: 'With *whom*? About *what* are you so upset?'

6. Comparative deletions

The standard of comparison is deleted.

❖   'This book is much better.'

ASK: 'Compared to what?'

Generalizations

We have also learned that information is generalized in three main ways:

1. Universal quantifiers

Generalizations that preclude any exceptions.

❖   'No one ever listens to me.'

ASK: 'Do you really mean *all* of the time; no one *ever* listens to you? Surely there might be some exceptions when someone somewhere has listened to you?'

2. Modal operator of necessity

Words that require particular action; the 'driver' word in the sentence if you like.

❖   Should
❖   Shouldn't
❖   Must
❖   Could
❖   Have to

ASK: What would happen if you did or didn't?

3. Modal operator of impossibility

These are just the opposite, words that imply no choice at all.

❖   Can't
❖   Haven't
❖   Won't

ASK: 'Just like before, what would happen if you did/didn't? Or, what's stopping you?'

Distortion

Finally, we learned that information is distorted in five main ways.

1. Complex equivalence

This is where two experiences are perceived as synonymous and often show up as two statements back to back.

❖ 'He left his socks on the floor again. He has no respect for me.'

ASK: 'How does doing X definitely mean Y?'

2. Lost performative

These are value judgements, rules and general opinions stated as fact, but the source of the assertion is missing.

❖ 'You need to drink eight glasses of water a day.'

ASK: 'Says *who*, or *how* do you know that, what happens if you don't?'

3. Mind-reading

This assumes that you know another person's internal state.

❖ 'They don't like change.'

ASK: '*How* do you know that?'

4. Cause and effect

This is the belief, or implication, that one person's actions or set of circumstances can cause another's emotional reaction.

❖ 'They made me do it.'

❖ 'I was stressed so I finished the bottle.'

ASK: '*How* does his/her/that doing/being X cause you to Y?'

5. Presuppositions

These are the basic assumptions that something must be true; it is presupposed that it *will* or *has* happened.

❖ 'Have they stopped being so grumpy?'

ASK: 'How do we know they were grumpy in the first place?' Or questions that uncover what may be taken for granted.

The very term 'distortions' strongly implies that we are making it up, or distorting something from the truth. Remember that there can be more than one truth. Often there's your truth, their truth and the truth. Avoid being seduced by your truth; don't just believe their truth, and instead get to 'the' truth. This means being as clean as possible in yourself and your own language first, and asking all the 'meta' questions when something doesn't make sense... Unless you are trying to persuade, in which case the reserve is true and you are trying to get someone to accept your truth. Use these skills with care and conscience though, as they are very powerful. Success comes from practise, and the best place to begin is with yourself.

Knowing What to Change

As you reach the end of this book, please know that you have actually only reached the end of the beginning for you. There is so much more to NLP than I have the scope or space to share here. Your mastery of NLP is going to take some practise, that's for sure. But, the good news is that all you need in order to practice are people, and there are plenty of those around.

The best opportunities to practise are when people don't know you're doing it – at least when you're building your observation and rapport skills, that is – as they'll generally be less guarded and much more genuine in their responses. When you are starting to think about using NLP to create change, start with yourself and then move on to others *only* with their express permission.

When you get really good at using the meta model (go on, which pattern was that?), you will be able to quickly and easily uncover what Richard Bandler calls 'the difference that makes the difference'. Most of the time, what we are looking for is not actually something new; it's something we've just not noticed before and in simply doing so, you immediately have the choice to change in a way you didn't even know was there.

Some of the other techniques you have learned in this book will help you to do that too but, in my experience, there is no substitute for hands-on proper training and experience working and learning with real people. While a book like this is a great place to start, trying to learn NLP without another human being present would be a bit like learning to cook using only a recipe book, but without ever chopping an onion or turning on an oven. No matter how brilliant the book, you simply need to get stuck in and get involved. It's a hands-on set of skills that you will pick up very quickly, but you do need to do that. If you'd like to take your NLP knowledge further then I strongly recommend a training course, and a face-to-face, hands-on one at that. There are plenty to choose from and the resources section at the back of the book will point you to what I believe are the best options.

NLP is a fantastic set of tools, principles, methodologies and models for enhancing communication and changing behaviour quickly and easily. But remember that NLP is in effect reverse-engineered from what happens naturally and what some highly effective people do without ever calling it NLP. So if you would like to create an enhanced version of yourself and enjoy the success that you hope it will bring then NLP is definitely a good home for you.

As you develop and study, you will be able to apply some of the techniques and principles you have learned here, and others, to change almost any unwanted behaviour. I'll resist the temptation to give you a big long list of all the issues, behaviours and applications where NLP can be very effective. I am resisting because I would like you to think about it in a much less prescriptive way and much more like a set of tools. A set of tools that with skill and practice you can use to change and build almost anything you want to. What you will be changing and building, of course, are states. As you know, **all behaviour is a product of the state of mind you are in at the time: different state, different choices, different outcome, different life**. It's as simple as that.

The one piece of guidance I would like to leave you with is this. While the change techniques here get all the plaudits, they are in fact only part of it. Finding and knowing what to change is the part that most people pay too little attention to and the best part is that if you pay enough attention the other person will often tell you what they already know they need to change. All change happens at a submodality level. Submodalities are after all the building blocks of any state and so the techniques are effectively ways to change large groups of submodalities all at once; you have to pay attention to know what to do, but that is all you have to do.

Case study

Ever heard the story of the giant ship engine that failed? The ship's owners tried one expert after another, but none of them could figure out how to fix the engine. Then they brought in an old man who had been fixing ships since he was a youngster. He carried a large bag of tools with him, and when he arrived, he immediately went to work. He inspected the engine very carefully, top to bottom.

Two of the ship's owners were there, watching this man, hoping he would know what to do. After looking things over, the old man reached into his bag and pulled out a small hammer. He gently tapped something. Instantly, the engine lurched into life. He carefully put his hammer away. The engine was fixed!

A week later, the owners received a bill from the old man for $10,000. 'What?' the owners exclaimed. 'He hardly did anything!' So they wrote the old man a note saying, 'Please send us an itemized bill.'

The man sent a bill that read:

Tapping with a hammer........... $2.00

Knowing where to tap............. $9998.00

The technique is important, but knowing where to make a change makes all the difference.

If you are working to help someone else then my advice is very simple. Pay close attention to the person in front of you and bring your own clean, clear and positive intention to the interaction. Pay attention to everything: eyes, language, mannerisms, actions and stay out of your own way. Leave your own stories behind and work with what's in front of you. If in doubt, ask. It's all there for you if you know where to tap.

References

1. James, W. *Principles of Psychology, Volume I* (Henry Holt, New York, 1890); 193–5

2. Kinsbourne, M. 'Eye and Head Turning Indicates Cerebral Lateralization', *Science,* 1972; 179: 539–41

3. Kocel, K. *et al.* 'Lateral Eye Movement and Cognitive Mode', *Psychon Sci*, 1972; 27: 223–4

4. Galin, D. and Ornstein, R. 'Individual Differences in Cognitive Style–Reflective Eye Movements', *Neuropsychologia*, 1974; 12: 376–97

5. Grinder, J., Bandler, R. and DeLozier, J. *Patterns of the Hypnotic Techniques of Milton H. Erickson, M.D. Volume II* (Meta Publications, California, 1977)

6. Dilts, R. *et al. NLP Volume I* (Meta Publications, California, 1980)

7. Dilts, R. *Roots of NLP* (Meta Publications, California, 1983)

8. Loiselle, F. 'The Effect of Eye Placement On Orthographic Memorization', Thesis, Faculte des Sciences Sociales, Universite de Moncton, New Brunswick, Canada, 1985

9. Buckner, W., Reese, E. and Reese, R. 'Eye Movement As An Indicator of Sensory Components in Thought', *Journal of Counseling Psychology*, 1987; (34)3

10. Bandler, R. and Grinder, J. *The Structure of Magic, Volume I* (Science and Behavior Books, 1989)

Resources

Books

Bandler, Richard. *Get the Life You Want*, Harper Element, 2009

Bandler, Richard. *How to Take Charge of Your Life: The User's Guide to NLP*, Harper Collins, 2014

Bandler, Richard. *An Insider's Guide to Submodalities*, Meta Publications, 1989

Bandler, Richard and Grinder, John. *Frogs into Princes*, Eden Grove Editions, 1990

Bandler, Richard and Grinder, John. *The Structure of Magic*, Volumes I and II, Science and Behavior Books, 1989

Bandler, Richard and Grinder, John. *Trance-formations*, Real People Press, 1981

Bandler, Richard, DeLozier, Judith and Grinder, John. *Patterns of the Hypnotic Techniques of Milton H. Erickson, M.D, Volumes I and II*, Meta Publications, 1975 and 1977; reprint editions, 1996

Dilts, Robert and Grinder, John. *Neurolinguistic Programming: The Study of the Structure of Subjective Experience, Volume I*, Meta Publications, 1989

Erickson, Milton H. and Rosen, Sidney. *My Voice Will Go with You: Teaching Tales of Milton H Erickson*, W.W. Norton & Company, 1991

Grinder, John and Pucelik, R. Frank. *The Origins of Neuro Linguistic Programmiing*, Crown House Publishing, 2013

Hall, L. Michael. *The Sourcebook of Magic: A Comprehensive Guide to NLP Change Patterns*, Crown House Publishing, 2003

Neill, Michael. *You Can Have What You Want*, Hay House UK, 2009

McKenna, Paul. *Change Your Life in 7 Days*, Bantam Press, 2010

Parker, Phil. *Get the Life You Love, Now*, Hay House UK, 2013

Satir, Virginia M. *The New Peoplemaking,* Science and Behavior Books, 1989

Websites

www.alicampbell.com to find out about my latest courses, how to book your place and what you can expect when you join me for some hands-on, cutting-edge training.

www.nlplifetraining.com for Richard Bandler NLP courses in the UK.

www.richardbandler.com for resources from the man himself.

www.purenlp.com for NLP courses worldwide.

http://www.philparker.org for some awesome NLP courses and resources in the UK.

Index

ABOUT THE AUTHOR

Ali Campbell is one of the world's leading life coaches. He has built an enviable reputation as a highly sought-after motivational coach, therapist, presenter and bestselling author. As a trusted advisor to celebrities, business leaders, sport stars, rock stars and even royalty, Ali is dubbed 'Mr Fix It', and is widely featured in the media – on television, radio and in print around the world.

The path to the life you want might be a lot easier than you think. You'll learn why past history is the worst possible predictor of your future, and how to navigate your own true path to whatever you want, no matter where you are starting out from. You may have heard that you have all the resources within you already, but that's not much use if you don't know how to find them and use them to achieve what you want. Ali is famed for being able to show you exactly how, and fast!

Ali's no-nonsense, irreverent style is like an arm around your shoulder and a kick up the butt, just when you need it. He gets to the point quickly and will have you laughing your way to achieving more in your life with a sense of peace and ease than you ever thought possible.

www.alicampbell.com

Listen. Learn. Transform.

Find fulfillment with unlimited Hay House audios!

Connect with your soul, step into your purpose, and embrace joy with world-renowned authors and teachers—all in the palm of your hand. With the *Hay House Unlimited* Audio app, you can learn and grow in a way that fits your lifestyle . . . and your daily schedule.

With your membership, you can:

- Expand your consciousness, reclaim your purpose, deepen your connection with the Divine, and learn to love and trust yourself fully.

- Explore thousands of audiobooks, meditations, immersive learning programs, podcasts, and more.

- Access exclusive audios you won't find anywhere else.

- Experience completely unlimited listening. No credits. No limits. No kidding.

Try for FREE!

Hay House Podcasts
Bring Fresh, Free Inspiration Each Week!

Hay House proudly offers a selection of life-changing audio content via our most popular podcasts!

Hay House Meditations Podcast

Features your favorite Hay House authors guiding you through meditations designed to help you relax and rejuvenate. Take their words into your soul and cruise through the week!

Dr. Wayne W. Dyer Podcast

Discover the timeless wisdom of Dr. Wayne W. Dyer, world-renowned spiritual teacher and affectionately known as "the father of motivation." Each week brings some of the best selections from the 10-year span of Dr. Dyer's talk show on Hay House Radio.

Hay House Podcast

Enjoy a selection of insightful and inspiring lectures from Hay House Live events, listen to some of the best moments from previous Hay House Radio episodes, and tune in for exclusive interviews and behind-the-scenes audio segments featuring leading experts in the fields of alternative health, self-development, intuitive medicine, success, and more! Get motivated to live your best life possible by subscribing to the free Hay House Podcast.

Listen on
Apple Podcasts

Find Hay House podcasts on iTunes, or visit
www.HayHouse.com/podcasts for more info.

HAY HOUSE

Look within

Join the conversation about latest products, events, exclusive offers and more.

 Hay House UK

 @HayHouseUK

 @hayhouseuk

 healyourlife.com

We'd love to hear from you!

Printed in the United States
by Baker & Taylor Publisher Services